Technological Change and Economic Performance

A large body of theoretical and empirical research has shown that technological change is a key determinant of economic performance.

This book provides a comprehensive review and synthesis of these "old" exogenous (Solow, Griliches, Jorgenson) and the "new" endogenous (Aghion, Romer, Helpman) growth studies. It also incorporates broader interdisciplinary perspectives on the measurement and analysis of economic performance, including:

- New methods for measuring productivity
- Recent interdisciplinary research on knowledge spillovers
- Reviews of recent papers on the Solow productivity paradox of computers, the role of "skill-biased" technological change, and the relationship between investment in technology and stock prices

This book is ideal for courses in economics, strategic management, science and technology policy, and technology management. It will also be extremely useful to technology managers, R&D employees, and technology consultants who want a parsimonious, mostly non-technical analysis of the policy implications of various new economy initiatives.

Albert N. Link is Professor of Economics at the University of North Carolina, Greensboro, USA and a Distinguished Special Professor at the Nottingham University Business School, UK.

Donald S. Siegel is Professor of Economics and Chair of the Economics Department at Rensselaer Polytechnic Institute, USA and a Visiting Professor at the Nottingham University Business School, UK.

Studies in Global Competition

A series of books edited by John Cantwell, The University of Reading, UK and David Mowery, University of California, Berkeley, USA

Japanese Firms in Europe
Edited by Frédérique Sachwald

Technological Innovation, Multinational Corporations and New International Competitiveness
The case of intermediate countries
Edited by José Molero

Global Competition and the Labour Market
Nigel Driffield

The Source of Capital Goods Innovation
The role of user firms in Japan and Korea
Kong-Rae Lee

Climates of Global Competition
Maria Bengtsson

Multinational Enterprises and Technological Spillovers
Tommaso Perez

Governance of International Strategic Alliances
Technology and transaction costs
Joanne E. Oxley

Strategy in Emerging Markets
Telecommunications establishments in Europe
Anders Pehrsson

Going Multinational
The Korean experience of direct investment
Edited by Frédérique Sachwald

Multinational Firms and Impacts on Employment, Trade and Technology
New perspectives for a new century
Edited by Robert E. Lipsey and Jean-Louis Mucchielli

Multinational Firms
The global–local dilemma
Edited by John H. Dunning and Jean-Louis Mucchielli

MIT and the Rise of Entrepreneurial Science
Henry Etzkowitz

Technological Resources and the Logic of Corporate Diversification
Brian Silverman

The Economics of Innovation, New Technologies and Structural Change
Cristiano Antonelli

European Union Direct Investment in China
Characteristics, challenges and perspectives
Daniel Van Den Bulcke, Haiyan Zhang and Maria do Céu Esteves

Biotechnology in Comparative Perspectives
Edited by Gerhard Fuchs

Technological Change and Economic Performance
Albert N. Link and Donald S. Siegel

Multinational Corporations and European Regional Systems of Innovation
John Cantwell and Simona Iammarino

Technological Change and Economic Performance

Albert N. Link and Donald S. Siegel

LONDON AND NEW YORK

First published 2003
by Routledge
2 Park Square, Milton Park, Abingdon, Oxfordshire OX14 4RN

Simultaneously published in the USA and Canada
by Routledge
711 Third Avenue, New York, NY 10017

Routledge is an imprint of the Taylor and Francis Group, an informa business

First issued in paperback 2015

© 2003 Albert N. Link and Donald S. Siegel

Typeset in Times New Roman by
Newgen Imaging Systems (P) Ltd, Chennai, India

All rights reserved. No part of this book may be reprinted or reproduced or utilized in any form or by any electronic, mechanical, or other means, now known or hereafter invented, including photocopying and recording, or in any information storage or retrieval system, without permission in writing from the publishers.

British Library Cataloguing in Publication Data
A catalogue record for this book is available from the British Library

Library of Congress Cataloging in Publication Data
Link, Albert N.
    Technological change and economic performance / Albert N. Link & Donald S. Siegel.
        p. cm. – (Studies in global competition ; v. 17)
    Updated ed. of: Technological change and productivity growth. c1987.
    Includes bibliographical references and index.
    1. Technological innovations – Economic aspects. 2. Industrial productivity. I. Siegel, Donald S., 1959– II. Link, Albert N. Technological change and productivity growth.
III. Title. IV. Series

HC79.T4 L56 2003
338′.064–dc21   2002035847

ISBN 978-0-415-27139-4 (hbk)
ISBN 978-1-138-81127-0 (pbk)

Contents

	List of figures	viii
	List of tables	ix
	Preface	xi
	Acknowledgments	xii
1	Introduction	1
2	Some preliminary concepts	5
3	Early theoretical and empirical studies of economic growth	13
4	The production function concept of technological change	20
5	Alternative frameworks for measuring technical progress and productivity	34
6	Trends in productivity growth	42
7	The productivity slowdown	49
8	Sources of technical knowledge	60
9	The technology–productivity growth relationship	70
10	Effects of information technology on workers and economic performance	79
11	Research partnerships and economic performance	98
12	Concluding statement	120
	Appendix A: Definition of symbols	121
	Appendix B: Stochastic frontier estimation	124
	Bibliography	126
	Index	149

Figures

4.1	Labor-saving, capital-saving, and neutral technological change with output held constant	21
8.1	Early conceptual model of sources of technical knowledge	60
8.2	An integrated look at the entrepreneurial process	63

Tables

3.1	Estimates of the rate of technological change	13
3.2	Comparison of old growth theory and new growth theory	18
5.1	Growth accounting components of growth in real gross US product	35
5.2	Selected studies examining the relationship between R&D expenditures and patent activity	37
5.3	Selected findings using patents as an output indicator	38
5.4	Selected studies of the diffusion of technology	39
6.1	Average annual growth rates in productivity measures in selected countries	43
6.2	Average annual growth rates in total factor productivity	44
6.3	Average annual growth rates in total factor productivity growth	45
6.4	Average annual growth rates in productivity measures in the US economy	46
6.5	Average annual growth rates in total factor productivity in US manufacturing industries	47
7.1	Average annual growth rates in productivity-related variables	52
8.1	Relative importance of alternative sources of technical knowledge	61
8.2	Relative importance of technical knowledge frequently used by R&D groups in US manufacturing firms	62
8.3	Selected studies of the relationship between innovation and firm size	68
8.4	Selected studies of knowledge spillovers	69
9.1	Summary of tax policies specific to R&D in various countries	74
9.2	Disaggregated R&D – productivity growth studies	75
9.3	Competitiveness of US industries in emerging technologies in the 1980s	77
10.1	Summary of empirical studies of skill-biased technological change	82
10.2	Summary of empirical studies of the relationship between computers and productivity growth	93

10.3	Sources of economic growth and computers	96
11.1	Recent empirical studies of the effects of research partnerships on economic performance	102
11.2	Summary of the policy literature related to the effects of research partnerships on economic performance	111

Preface

This volume is an updated version of Link's 1987 monograph, *Technological Change and Productivity Growth*. It appears that there is much to update and extend, given the burgeoning literature on new growth theory and renewed interest in explaining the determinants of overall economic growth. There has also been the development of new empirical methods to assess the relationship between technological change and productivity growth and economic performance, as well as recognition that technological change is often accompanied by organizational changes that can have an influence on economic performance. Each of these topics is considered in great detail in this volume.

This volume, like the 1987 monograph, begins by presenting some basic analytical concepts related to technological change and productivity growth that provide the foundation for this body of literature. Greater availability of microeconomic data sets and increased computing power has resulted in a surge of empirical work on technological change and productivity growth. Unfortunately, it appears that many newly minted PhDs are ignoring much of the pioneering foundation work in this field, especially in the old growth theory literature. This is due, in part, to the fact that they may not have been exposed to this work. Furthermore, there has been no systematic attempt to link the old and new growth theory literatures. We attempt to fill this gap in this volume.

Acknowledgments

This book has benefited from the advice and assistance of many individuals. Special thanks are due to Mike Scherer for his extensive comments on the 1987 monograph, *Technological Change and Productivity Growth*, upon which this volume is based.

We are also indebted to the late Zvi Griliches, the late Ed Mansfield, David Audretsch, Kathy Combs, Maryann Feldman, Bronwyn Hall, Cathy Morrison Paul, and John Scott for insightful comments regarding the "new" literature on technological change and economic performance. Thanks also to Rob Langham and Terry Clague at Routledge, who have been extremely helpful and patient in the preparation of this volume.

Lastly, but most importantly, we thank our wives, Carol and Sandra, and our children, Jamie and Kevin, and Joshua, William, and Shira, for providing the warmth and emotional sustenance that made this book possible.

1 Introduction

Productivity growth is vital to economic well-being or economic growth because it enhances standards of living as well as the quality of life. Productivity growth improves economic efficiency, meaning the ability of firms to produce more output at all levels of existing inputs. Economic efficiency leads to increases in income – personal, state, and national – that can then be used for additional consumption and for improvements in social conditions, such as reductions in relative poverty and environmental pollution and improvements in the quality of health care.

The point to be emphasized is that productivity growth ultimately leads to an improvement in the quality of life. Furthermore, it also enhances a nation's global competitiveness, reduces inflationary pressures, and thus fosters overall economic stability. Finally, productivity growth stimulates market competition within a domestic economy but more importantly it does so within the global marketplace. Thus, productivity growth improves the efficiency of resource allocation.

One factor responsible for productivity growth is technological change, or technical progress. Technological change results in an improvement in the efficiency of production, which in turn leads to productivity growth. And, as just stated, productivity growth improves economic efficiency and ultimately enhances overall economic growth. To understand better the concept of productivity growth both for academic as well as policy-related reasons – and the policy reasons are obvious from the connection between productivity growth and overall economic growth – it is imperative to understand first the nature of technological changes and the linkages between technological change and productivity growth.

The importance of technological change or technical progress and economic growth has long been discussed in the economics literature. Traditionally, scholars have referred to the first chapter in Adam Smith's (1937) *An Inquiry into the Nature and Causes of the Wealth of Nations* in order to motivate their discussion regarding the relationship between technological change and economic growth. For Smith, innovation is the product of division of labor, and division of labor in turn depends on the extent of the market. It is innovation – which many scholars today mistakenly associate as being synonymous with technological change, and innovation will be shown herein to be a necessary precursor to technological change – that leads to economic growth. Smith's innovator, his philosopher or speculator, was an amateur by today's modern standards, but Smith's view of innovation as a professional activity was indeed ahead of its time.

Contemporary academic interest in the topics related to technological change and economic growth, stems in large part from Smith, but also from a rich history of economic thought about the entrepreneur. As chronicled by Hébert and Link (1988), the crucial role of the entrepreneur in economic theory was first and foremost recognized by Richard Cantillon (1931), whose *Essai Sur la Nature du Commerce en Général* was published posthumously in 1755. Cantillon's entrepreneur is someone who engages in exchange for profit. Specifically, he or she is someone who exercises judgment in the face of uncertainty. François Quesnay (1888), the singular leader of the French Physiocrats, built on Cantillon's ideas but did not further the Cantillon notion of the entrepreneur. To Quesnay, the entrepreneur was little more than a manager or independent owner of a business.

Among Quesnay's disciples was Abbé Nicolas Baudeau (1910) who, in his 1867 treaties *Premier Introduction à la Philosophie E'conomique*, wrote that the sources of economic growth fall into two categories: those sources that are subject to human control and thereby depend on knowledge and ability, and those that do not. It was Baudeau's entrepreneur who exercised intelligence to combine ideas in order to bring about innovations, and thereby to influence economic growth.

Contemporary policy interest in topics related to technological change and productivity growth, stems for the most part from the fact that economic growth is of overarching policy concern, but not to be dismissed from an understanding of the policy interest in technological change are the findings from a large body of economic research on the relationship between technological change and productivity growth that flourished during the mid- to late 1950s. This body of research concluded that technological change was the most important single factor associated with aggregate economic growth. This conclusion represented a major shift in thinking about the sources of economic growth, as opposed to the *per se* importance of economic growth. The conventional wisdom at that time held that economic growth resulted from the use of more inputs, especially physical capital, and the growth of physical capital was the primary determinant of enhancements in economic growth. Instead, the empirical evidence from studies during the mid- to late 1950s appeared to suggest that it was not the scale or amount of inputs but the efficiency with which inputs were used that was the most important factor driving improvements in economic performance. And, the efficiency with which inputs are used comes from improvements in the utilization of knowledge or technological change.

Partly as a result of the findings of these early studies, which are discussed in detail in later chapters in this volume, an academic as well as policy-relevant body of literature began to emerge. This literature focused on the relationship between technological change and productivity growth, and as well extended the economic foundations upon which the relationship between the two concepts could be explained. This body of thought is what we refer to throughout this volume as the old growth theory literature, as opposed to more recent new growth theory literature.

Therefore, one area of emphasis in this volume is the evolution of thought on technological change, productivity growth, and economic performance. Our purpose in presenting this material, and in so emphasizing those topics, is to provide a bridge between the old and new growth theory literatures.

Regarding the old growth theory literature, it is important to note that there was considerable interest in economic policies to promote economic growth in the aftermath of the devastation of the Second World War. The high rates of economic growth achieved by the OECD nations in the 1950s and 1960s appeared to be a confirmation of the success of the post-war policies to promote industrial development, in part through increased research and development (R&D), as a means to enhance technological progress and thus economic performance. However, the worldwide slowdown in productivity growth that began in the late 1960s, and which was exacerbated in the early 1970s and extended into the 1980s, appeared to have revived academic interest as well as policy interest in these topics.

The remaining chapters in this volume trace the development of thought, meaning more specifically the development of economic models and their empirical counterparts, on these myriad issues. As an overview, Chapter 2 sets the stage for the remainder of the volume by discussing some preliminary concepts such as technological change, productivity growth, and economic performance. Chapter 3, building on the concepts in Chapter 2, overviews the early and foundationally important studies on productivity growth. Implicit in the discussions in Chapters 2 and 3 is the notion of a production function. Chapter 4 deals with the measurement of technological change within a production function framework. Alternative frameworks for conceptualizing about and measuring technological change are discussed in Chapter 5. In Chapter 6, historical trends in productivity growth are documents and discussed with an eye toward economic performance and hence toward technology-based economic growth policy. Chapter 7 revisits the productivity slowdown that occurred in most industrial nations in the 1960s and early 1970s within the context of the production function framework developed in Chapters 2, 3, and 4. We present this material, with an eye towards generating lessons to be learned for structuring technology-based growth policy. This background information logically leads to Chapter 8 and the development of a framework for conceptualizing about the sources of technological change. Chapter 9 extends this framework and also considers policy-relevant applications. Chapter 10 discusses much of the new literature on the effects of information technology on workers and economic performance using the frameworks presented in previous chapters. Chapter 11 uses these same conceptual frameworks to focus on the relationship between research partnerships and economic performance.

The extant literature is summarized in the above chapters in a variety of ways. As stated and rationalized in the Preface, we emphasize the pioneering research in the field of technological and productivity growth. Thus, many of the foundation works are summarized and elaborated upon in tables. Where appropriate, we summarize a body of literature in terms of overall conclusions or in terms of details about particular research contributions. Since Link's 1987 monograph detailed much of the early literature, as others have done since, the summary tables are intentionally brief and to the point. The material in Chapters 10 and 11 represents the most recent body of thought on the topics herein, as such that literature is detailed in greater detail in the summary tables. Chapter 12 concludes the volume in a prospective manner, proposing a selected agenda for additional research and policy initiatives.

2 Some preliminary concepts

The concepts of technological change and productivity growth, which were introduced, but only briefly discussed in Chapter 1, have become commonplace in the vocabulary of those who analyze the economics of science and technology. However, as the title of this volume implies, there is also a critical relationship between technological change and economic performance.

When economists proffer science- and technology-based policy recommendations, they focus their attention on policies that have the potential to increase economic performance. That is not surprising, since economists believe that the primary role of public policy is to enhance economic welfare. Likewise, when policy makers choose among policy alternatives their attention focuses on the economic performance enhancing potential of each initiative in their choice set. Such a focus thus dictates consistency in the use of the underlying concepts.

In this chapter we analyze three related concepts: technological change, productivity growth, and economic performance. Our purpose for beginning with these first principles is twofold. First, we seek to ground the reader in concepts that are fundamental for the remaining chapters. Second, we also want to contribute to the broader academic literature in this regard, since these first principles are frequently ignored. Furthermore, we hope that the discussion that follows may also help to provide some consistency in thought, and therefore in policy, about fundamental issues in science and technology policy.

Technology and technological change

Researchers have used the concept of technology in a variety of ways. In a narrow sense, technology refers to specific physical or tangible tools, but in a broader sense technology describes whole social processes. In the broader sense, technology refers to intangible tools. Although there are analytical advantages to both the narrow and the more encompassing views, the different uses of the concept of technology invariably promote confusion at both the theoretical, empirical, and policy levels.

A concept of technology that embraces social or intangible entities is beyond the scope of the discussion in this volume. Although important, concepts such as technological ethic or organizational technology are not directly aligned with the productivity growth, technological change, economic performance paradigm that will be developed in the following chapters. And, equally as important, and rightly or wrongly, these eschewed concepts do not have a place in mainstream economic thought. Instead, taking the road most traveled, we proceed to focus on the narrow view of technology.

By focusing on physical or tangible technology, some problems still remain. By focusing on physical technology, questions arise such as: How can technologies be differentiated? What aspects of technology are of interest? For the most part, economists have attempted to answer such questions by dealing with the indirectly perceivable aspects of physical technology or tangible tools. Namely, the focus turns from attributes to the knowledge embodied within the technology. And, the knowledge base of technology is not only a theme upon which we dwell herein, but also it is a critically important starting point for the development of science and technology policy.

Conceptualizing technology as the physical representation of knowledge provides a useful foundation for understanding technological change and its determinants. Any useful device is, in part, proof of the knowledge-based or informational assumptions that resulted in its creation. The information embodied in a technology varies accordingly to its source, its type, and its application. For example, one source of information is science, although scientific knowledge is rarely sufficient for the more particular needs entailed in constructing, literally, a technological device. Having said that, it would be useful in this regard to think of science as focusing on the understanding of knowledge and technology as focusing on the application of knowledge.

Other sources of knowledge include information from controlled and random experimentation, information that philosophers refer to as ordinary knowledge, and finally, information of the kind that falls under the rubrics of creativity, perceptiveness, and inspiration. Regarding perceptiveness, Machlup (1980: 179) argued that formal education is only one form of knowledge. He asserted that knowledge is also gained experientially and is gathered and processed at different rates by each individual. The following statement reflects Machlup's notion of perception quite clearly:

> Some alert and quick-minded persons, by keeping their eyes and ears open for new facts and theories, discoveries and opportunities, perceive what normal people of lesser alertness and perceptiveness, would fail to notice. Hence new knowledge is available at little or no cost to those who are on the lookout, full of curiosity, and bright enough not to miss their chances.

This informational view of technology implies that technology *per se* is an output that arises from a formal, rational, purposively undertaken process. Such an idea – the production of technology – highlights the role of research in the generation of technologies. And, the concept of research underscores the myriad sources available from which knowledge can be acquired. Technologies can thus be distinguished, albeit imperfectly, by the amount of embedded information.

More concretely, R&D activities – wherever they are based – play a large role in creating and characterizing new technologies.

Closely related to the concept of technology is the notion of invention and innovation. One useful distinction between the two is to associate newness with invention and usefulness with innovation. So doing defines an innovation as an invention put into practice. But, there remains a terminological problem even at this general level: Does new refer to something new in the world, or to something new to the user? We view newness in terms of an invention being brought into being and an innovation being brought into use. The characteristics of newness appear in the writing of many scholars who attempted to address this topic. Kuznets (1962: 19), for example, refers to inventive activity as a "new combination of available knowledge."

For the purposes at hand, it may be useful to think of an invention as the creation of a new technology. Innovation, then, is the first application of the invention – the technology – in production. Scherer's (1965*b*) study of the Watt–Boulton steam-engine venture supports this relationship between invention and innovation in the process of technological change. Since innovation or application implies the beginning of a diffusion process, the conceptualizations parallel the Schumpeterian idea that there are phases in the process of technological change: invention, innovation, diffusion, and imitation.

Schumpeter's contribution to the history of economic thought on entrepreneurship, innovation, and economic growth in the early and mid-1900s has significantly influenced how many economists and other scholars and researchers approach the broader topic of technological change and economic performance. According to Schumpeter (1939: 62), innovation can meaningfully be defined in terms of a production function, and, in a sense, as a factor shifting the production function:

> [The production function] describes the way in which quantity of product varies if quantities of factors vary. If, instead of quantities of factors, we vary the form of the function, we have an innovation.

He noted that mere cost-reducing applications of knowledge lead only to new supply schedules of existing goods. Therefore, this kind of innovation must involve a new commodity or one of a higher quality. This is what economists typically refer to as product innovation. Schumpeter also noted that the knowledge undergirding the innovation need not be new; it may be existing knowledge that has not been utilized before. According to Schumpeter (1928: 378):

> [T]here never has been anytime when the store of scientific knowledge has yielded all it could in the way of industrial improvement, and, on the other hand, it is not the knowledge that matters, but the successful solution of the task *sui generis* of putting an untried method into practice – there may be, and often is, no scientific novelty involved at all, and even if it be involved, this does not make any difference to the nature of the process.

8 *Some preliminary concepts*

More than two decades after these writings of Schumpeter, Usher (1954) independently rediscovered these same concepts. He posited that technology is the result of an innovation, and an innovation is the result of an invention. An invention, of course, results as the emergence of new things requiring an act of insight going beyond the normal exercise of technical or professional skills.

Productivity and productivity growth

There are numerous definitions of productivity and productivity growth, and for each definition there are many ways to measure the constructs. The most common definition begins with a traditional economic representation – known as a production function – of a relationship between inputs and an output.

Throughout this volume many functional forms are presented. For reference purposes, many of the symbols that are used are again defined in Appendix A.

Within a production function framework, productivity can be thought of as the degree of efficiency exhibited in the process of transforming inputs into an output. If output, Q, and a vector of n inputs $(x_1, \ldots, x_n)$, denoted by X, are related as:

$$Q = A f(X) \tag{2.1}$$

A is considered to be a shift factor that captures the degree of efficiency exhibited in the production process. We also assume, and so note, at least for the time being, that there is no time dimension to A. If firm 1 is more efficient in the process of transforming inputs into an output than firm 2, even though both firms rely on the same production inputs, then firm 1 is said to be more productive than firm 2. It thus follows that firm 1's output is greater than firm 2's output, given the same vector of n inputs. Based on the production function in equation (2.1), equation (2.2) denotes that firm 1 is more productive than firm 2, at a given point in time, as:

$$\{Q_1 = A_1 f(X)\} > \{Q_2 = A_2 f(X)\}. \tag{2.2}$$

The concept of firm 1 being more productive or having greater productivity than firm 2 can also be addressed using a dual approach based within a cost-function framework. A cost function is a relationship between the price of each of the individual inputs used in the underlying production process and the total cost associated with producing output from that process. To draw a parallel to equation (2.1), a cost function is a relationship between the total cost of production, C, and the output being produced, Q, as:

$$C = H g(Q), \tag{2.3}$$

where, ignoring for the moment the price of inputs, H is a shift factor, analogous to A in equation (2.1), capturing cost efficiency. Firm 1 is said to be more productive than firm 2 if firm 1's total cost of production is less than firm 2's, given the same level of output. Based on the total cost function in equation (2.3), equation (2.4), which parallels equation (2.2), signifies that firm 1 is more productive than firm 2, at a given point in time, as:

$$\{C_1 = H_1 \, g(Q)\} < \{C_2 = H_2 \, g(Q)\}. \tag{2.4}$$

However, it is important to emphasize that while equations (2.2) and (2.4) represent similar concepts, there is an important economic distinction between the economic foundation of the two measures. On the one hand, a production function-based measure of productivity, based on equation (2.1), captures a firm's technical efficiency in transforming inputs into output; a production function is theoretically based on physical productivity. On the other hand, a cost function-based measure of productivity, based on equation (2.3), captures a firm's relative cost efficiency in transforming inputs into output. That is, production and cost functions are each based on a notion of optimality. The former represents the combinations of inputs that generate the most output, given the current state of technology. The latter denotes the least-cost combinations of these inputs that generate any given level of output, given the current state of technology.

While productivity in the comparative sense of the production relationships in equation (2.2) – that is, comparing the productivity of firm 1 to firm 2 – is important and will be discussed again in greater detail, the literature, specially the empirical literature, on productivity and productivity growth began at the macroeconomic level but has evolved in terms of more microeconomic units of analysis – a plant, a firm, an industry – as will be shown below. Thus, continuing with the production-function approach, equation (2.1) can be rewritten as:

$$Q = A(t) f(X), \tag{2.5}$$

where $A(t)$ is a time-related shift factor and where t indexes time. Given the specification in equation (2.5), the productivity of the relationship between all inputs and output – or more appropriately referred to as total factor productivity, *TFP* – over time can be represented by simply rearranging the terms, as:

$$TFP = A(t) = Q / f(X) \tag{2.6}$$

As a historical aside, in the 1930s the economics literature first began to acknowledge that labor was not the only factor of production, but that capital and land were also both important (Griliches 1996). That is, it was recognized that productivity measures should take account of all the relevant factors of production. Equation (2.6) is, following Copeland (1937), a productivity ratio. And, since the vector X captures all inputs, equation (2.6) is an output-over-total inputs index of productivity.

The earliest efforts to measure such an index of total factor-productivity growth trace to Tinbergen (1942) and Stigler (1947); others' measurement efforts are discussed in later chapters. One lasting result from the focus of Copeland,

Tinbergen, and Stigler was a change in emphasis from labor productivity, which was widely regarded to be the most valid metric of economic efficiency, to total factor productivity.

Vector X, as previously noted, represents all inputs used in the production process, $(x_1, \ldots, x_n)$. Partial factor productivity is a productivity index specific to one input, say input x_i, written as (Q/x_i). Because not all inputs contribute equally to the production of output, total factor productivity in equation (2.4) can be expanded and rewritten as:

$$TFP = A(t) = Q / f(X) = Q / \sum w_i x_i \qquad (2.7)$$

where each of the x_i inputs has a separate and distinct contribution, and is therefore weighted by a separate and distinct individual input weight, w_i, $(0 \leq w_i \leq 1)$.

Following from equation (2.7), the concept of technological change can refer to the percentage rate of growth over time of total factor productivity, written as:

$$\frac{\partial TFP/\partial t}{TFP} = \frac{\partial A(t)/\partial t}{A(t)} = \frac{A'}{A} \qquad (2.8)$$

where, again for notational simplicity, the time notation on $A(t)$ is frequently dropped and where $A' = \partial A(t)/\partial t$.

Economic performance

The concept of economic performance, like the concepts of productivity and technology, has been defined in numerous ways in economics and in related disciplines. Not surprisingly and quite acceptably, scholars in different academic fields define economic performance in terms of their own genre of concepts.

Before defining the concept of economic performance, the issue of aggregation must be mentioned. It is somewhat appealing, at least for many academics and most policy makers, to think of economic performance at the aggregate level and specifically in terms of an aggregate production function. However, from a policy perspective the appropriate level of aggregation might not be the nation but rather the industry or sector. Still, as with most economic concepts, there is a trade-off between one's comfort with a concept and either the accuracy with which that concept can be measured or the relevance of the concept to policy.

As a general rule when dealing with technological change, productivity growth, and economic performance, measurement problems increase with the level of aggregation. As will be discussed in later chapters, much of the early literature on productivity growth was at the national level or sectoral level. While measurement problems were realized by most scholars, problems were often set aside in favor of the interpretative value and presumed policy importance of such aggregated analysis.

As more microeconomic data sets have become available to researchers for analysis, the level of aggregation in economic research has accordingly become more microeconomic in nature. It is not surprising then that many scholars today address economic performance – especially economic performance that is technology based – at the individual, plant, or firm level where measurement problems can be addressed with some degree of accuracy. Several measures of economic performance are noted below, but each will also be discussed in detail in later chapters with reference to the extant literature.

At the microeconomic level, one measure of the economic performance of a firm relates to the market value of the firm's patents. More productive firms, especially those whose productivity is technology based, will enjoy greater market value for their generated knowledge as captured by the market value of their patents.

Another measure of economic performance relates to the market's acceptance of a firm's innovation as measured in terms of how the innovation diffuses through the applicable industries. And relatedly, diffusion rates also proxy this aspect of economic performance. Of course, from a financial perspective, both of these concepts of economic performance are related to accounting profitability.

Regarding accounting profitability, although accounting profitability as a measure of economic performance lacks the same economic tradition as an output measure from a production function, a profit function can be represented similarly. A firm's profit, Π, function is written as a function of its output as:

$$\Pi = P\, h(Q), \tag{2.9}$$

where P is a shift factor, and again where time is not specified for notational simplicity. Firm 1 is said to perform better, that is more profitably, than firm 2 if firm 1's economic profit is greater than firm 2's, given the same level of output. Firm 1 is more profitable than firm 2, as:

$$\{\Pi_1 = P_1\, h(Q)\} > \{\Pi_2 = P_2\, h(Q)\}. \tag{2.10}$$

From a financial market perspective, economic performance can also be defined in terms of a firm's share price, meaning the market-determined value of an ownership share in a publicly owned firm. If firm 1's stock market value (number of shares outstanding multiplied by the average share price) is greater than firm 2's, *ceteris paribus*, then it follows that the market values the current, or expected future, economic performance of firm 1 is more than firm 2. Reliance on share price to define the economic performance of a firm is appealing on several grounds. First, it obviates the need to deal with difficult measurement issues associated with the measurement of partial factor or total factor productivity. Second, inputs and output, costs, and profit are variables that can be influenced by the discretion of management in pursuit of their own goals and objectives rather than the economic objectives of the firm. Share price is much more difficult, if not impossible, for managers to manipulate.

Relatedly, economic performance has also been defined in terms of long-run market stock price effects. The conceptual notion is that the long-run market stock price will reflect the value of more productive or more efficient firms.

In addition to these measures of economic performance, others have appeared from time to time in the literature. For example, differences in labor productivity are, *ceteris paribus*, reflected in differences in wages or compensation, assuming of course that labor is paid the value of its marginal product. Likewise, effective individual investments in knowledge – human capital – to enhance one's productivity capabilities will be revealed, and valued, by the market in terms of higher wages or compensation.

Although not addressed in the academic literature, we posit that the benefits or returns to society from technological change also represent a valid measure of economic performance. Whereas a firm's private rate of return from its investments in R&D, say, is embedded in a firm's accounting profit or its share price, a social rate of return from society's investments in R&D, say, are less tractable even though the R&D investing firm is part of society. Nevertheless, we will argue that such a measure of economic performance has merit especially in cases where publicly financed R&D is involved.

3 Early theoretical and empirical studies of economic growth

Formal studies relating technological change to productivity growth blossomed in the 1970s, possibly in response to the pervasive slowdown in productivity growth that occurred during this period. While the early post-Second World War researchers perceived the fundamental importance of technological change as an underlying force for productivity growth and thus for economic performance, their writings were less formal than those of their disciples. Nelson (1981: 1030) perceptively observed that these early writers were "remarkable in foreshadowing the central conclusion of studies done somewhat later within the neoclassical framework."

An overview of the early studies

A number of post-Second World War researchers are selectively referenced in Table 3.1, along with the key findings from their investigations. Each researcher noted in the table used a variant of an output-over-all inputs index to construct a productivity index, and then to estimate so-measured increases in output, holding the quantity of inputs fixed. That is, each researcher estimated increases in resource efficiency. Presumably, these measured efficiency gains were, in part, the result

Table 3.1 Estimates of the rate of technological change, derived from seminal post-war studies of the US economy

Author	Time period	Measure of economic performance	Estimated average annual rate of technological change (in percent)
Schmookler (1952)	1869–78 to 1929–38	GNP per unit of input	1.36
Mills (1952)	1891–1900 to 1941–50	GNP per manhour	3.6
Schultz (1953)	1910 to 1950	Agriculture output per unit input	0.8 to 1.35
Kendrick (1956)	1899 to 1953	Private domestic output per unit of input	1.7
Solow (1957)	1909 to 1949	GNP per unit of labor	1.5

of economy-wide technological advances, a point that most researchers speculated about at that time, but did not formally quantify.

In addition to those listed in the table, Abramovitz (1956), in his hallmark study, examined economic activity in the post-Civil war economy, from 1869–78 to 1944–53. He cautiously concluded from his quantitative investigation that the source of growth in output per unit of labor over that time period was not increased resources per head. Rather, the source of growth in output per unit of labor rested within the realm of such a little-understood cause as the growth in the stock of knowledge. It is no wonder, then, that Abramovitz (1956) coined the descriptive phrase, "measure of ignorance," when referring to the determinants of productivity growth. He conjectured that the inputs into this stock of knowledge included such factors as research and education – both of which are bases for the generation of new knowledge.

Solow (1957) was the first to formalize the study of productivity growth within the context of an aggregate production function model of the form in equation (2.5). His pioneering model will be developed fully in Chapter 4. Solow's empirical analysis, applied to the US economy for the period 1909 to 1949, led him to conclude, much like writers before him had done, that technological change was a critically important source of US economic growth. Specifically, Solow (1957: 320) concluded, "gross output per man-hour doubled over the [time] interval, with 87½ percent of the increase attributable to technical change."

Solow realized that his empirical result and interpretative conclusion compared closely with that of Fabricant (1954) from a few years before. Fabricant had also estimated that about 90 percent of the increase in output per capita between 1871 and 1951 was attributable to technical progress, but he did not do so within a production function model.

The quantitative research that followed from these early empirical studies had two objectives. One objective was to understand and refine the aggregate production-function model posited by Solow, which was expected at that time to be able to result in more accurate estimates of the impact of technological change on economic activity. A second objective was to improve the quality of input measures used to calculate productivity indices, as well as to expand the set of inputs considered. Both of these related areas of emphasis ultimately focused on understanding economic performance, of which economic growth was of primary emphasis. Thus, before reviewing this literature, it is important to have a historical understanding of how economic growth, as conceptualized and measured in these investigations, fits within two larger bodies of theoretical literature, old growth theory and new growth theory.

Old growth theory

It is critical to note that much of the theoretical work that falls under the heading of old growth theory was driven by the availability of data. That is, the development of National Income and Product Accounts, and other macroeconomic data sets on output and input usage in the early 1950s, was a major breakthrough that influenced the development of this body of theory. These data sets came about largely due to the influence of Kuznets and other scholars affiliated with the National Bureau of Economic Research, which was then located in New York City. The empirical studies cited in Table 3.1 were all attempts to measure and explain sources of economic growth over time. The authors referenced in the table used basically the same approach in their efforts to account for sources of economic growth. That is, the total contribution of input growth was computed by weighting each input – capital and labor – by their relative prices. As noted by Griliches (1996), this weighting of inputs seemed like such an obvious thing to do that no one felt compelled at that time to justify it theoretically.

The latter fact – that is, the widespread acceptance of weighting inputs – explains why Solow's 1957 article is regarded today as the seminal article in the field. Solow was the first to explicitly tie residual growth, A'/A in equation (2.8), to the formal neoclassical growth theory that he had previously set forth in his 1956 article. A similar growth theoretic model was independently exposited in a contemporary study by Swan (1956). These two theoretical advancements by Solow and Swan can be construed as an example within the annals of economics, along with Adam Smith's pin factory, where empirical observation such as those in Table 3.1 led to a major theoretical contribution.

The articles by Solow (1956) and Swan (1956) formed the basis of what was then considered to be modern growth theory but which is now referred to as old growth theory. Solow and Swan drew heavily from the works by Harrod (1946) and Domar (1947), parts of which are discussed in Chapter 4. As McCallum (1996: 11) points out:

> Solow's contribution was great, nevertheless, because he (and Swan) developed something that might reasonably be called a *model*, whereas Harrod and Domar had only derived (via elementary algebra) a *condition* that needed to be satisfied for steady growth.

In any event, the early old growth theory models all made a number of simplifying interrelated assumptions regarding producer behavior and factor markets. Specifically, these models assumed that perfect competition characterizes both input and output markets; production is characterized by constant returns to scale; and factors are paid their social marginal products. The latter assumption implies that factor markets are perfectly competitive and all externalities are captured by the firm's behavior.

Looking ahead to the reasoning of many scholars who reflected on the well-known importance of knowledge as a source of innovation and innovation as a source for technological change, one obvious contradiction is present in these old growth theory models. It is well known that under prefect competition firms have little incentive to invest in R&D, an investment activity that will be the focal point in much of the technology–productivity growth relationship literature discussed in Chapter 9. Furthermore, investments in knowledge *per se* typically entail substantial up-front costs, and for such costs to be incurred it follows that that there must be increasing returns to scale and output prices must be greater than the marginal cost of production otherwise the knowledge investment costs would not be recovered. These conditions, of course, violate the assumptions of perfect competition and constant returns to scale.

Two other results in Solow's (1956) growth model have also troubled many economists, even at the time when his article was first published. Following Nelson (1997), these concerns were and still are that technological change was modeled as an exogenous event and that changes in the saving rate were modeled to have no lasting effect on the rate of growth of output per worker. While certainly simplifying, the concept of technological change falling on firms like manna from heaven was problematic since it seemed fairly obvious, even at that time, that R&D was the result of purposive activity and that innovative behavior varied in response to such activities. As an aside, these are points that seem obvious to contemporary scholars in this field, although these ideas also follow logically from the writings of the Physiocrats nearly a century before.

Solow (1956) also hypothesized that diminishing returns to capital implied that the economy's steady-state growth rate would be independent of its savings rate. As noted by Nelson (1997), this was a finding that many thought to be the most implausible.

Although some economists questioned the basic assumptions of the Solow model, a quiet consensus still emerged around this production function framework in the 1960s and early 1970s, and as a result, there were few advances in growth theory for several decades. Furthermore, the oil price shocks and the resulting economic slowdown in productivity growth in the early 1970s diverted the attention of economists to a debate on energy-capital substitution and the factors influencing business-cycle fluctuations. While the productivity growth slowdown of the late 1960s and early 1970s and 1980s did generate more interest in the determinants of long-run growth, it was the debate regarding convergence in rates of economic growth across countries, which followed directly from the Solow (1956) model, that served as the catalyst for stimulating new theoretical research on growth.

Jorgenson (1996), among others, noted that much of the empirical evidence of the day on growth rates was not consistent with convergence. More specifically, Jorgensen pointed out that Solow's (1956) assumption of diminishing marginal returns to capital results in a growth process within a country in which it eventually reaches a steady state of per capital income growth. This steady-state rate is hypothesized to be determined by several factors: the share of capital in Gross Domestic Product (GDP), population growth, productivity growth, and the rate of depreciation of capital equipment. Using widely accepted values for each of these parameters, Jorgenson concluded that the actual rate of convergence is too low to be consistent with Solow's model.

New growth theory

The anomalous finding discussed by Jorgenson (1996) stimulated researchers, such as Romer (1986), to question the underlying assumptions of the neoclassical growth model. Romer's initial work is generally regarded as the key initial contribution to new growth theory. Romer concluded that because the evidence on the slow rate of convergence was not consistent with the neoclassical growth theory, Solow's (1956) growth model needed to be revisited. Romer proposed allowing for increasing returns to scale in the aggregate production function and externalities arising from private capital investment to the rest of the economy. We contend that Romer's work is also more general in the sense that it refers to accumulation, which can mean accumulation of knowledge, physical capital, or human capital. Similar assumptions were also made in a highly influential new growth theory article by Lucas (1988), although he focused specifically on the role of human capital.

Romer's (1990) subsequent work treated technological change as an endogenous factor of growth. This was an obvious departure from old growth theory, as well as an important extension of the literature on technological change and productivity growth since he outlined a highly stylized equilibrium model in which agents engaging in R&D optimize. Aghion and Howitt (1990), Grossman and Helpman (1991a,b), and Klette and Griliches (1997) also delineated models in which firms engage in R&D. In Aghion and Howitt (1990), technological change is treated as an endogenous process of creative destruction, where new technologies displace old technologies.

As noted earlier, the role of the entrepreneur as a key player in economics and the concept of creative destruction were discussed in previous literatures. Indeed, these concepts have a rich tradition in the history of economic thought, and one that is fundamental to understanding the endogenous nature of technological change. Following Hébert and Link (1988), for Schumpeter (1934), as outlined in his *Theory of Economic Development*, competition involved mainly the dynamic innovation of the entrepreneur, as was noted herein in Chapter 2. He used the concept of equilibrium as a theoretical construct or point of departure. The chief characteristic of the equilibrium state, or the circular flow of economic life as he also called it, is to emphasize that economic life proceeds routinely on the basis of past experience. Within this equilibrium system, the production function is invariant although factor substitution is possible within the limits of known technological horizons. The only real function that must be performed in this state, according to Schumpeter (1934: 45), is:

> that of combining the two original factors of production, and this function is performed in every period mechanically as it were, of its own accord, without requiring a personal element distinguishable from superintendence and similar things.

In this artificial situation the entrepreneur is a nonentity without a special function. The relevant problem, according to Schumpeter (1950), as articulated in *Capitalism, Socialism and Democracy*, is not how capitalism administers existing structures but how it creates and destroys them. This is the process that Schumpeter called creative destruction, and it is the essence of economic growth.

18 *Early theoretical and empirical studies of economic growth*

In other words, economic growth comes from a disturbance of the equilibrium state. It is a process defined by carrying out new combinations in production; it is accomplished by the entrepreneur.

In the Romer (1990) tradition, Grossman and Helpman (1991a,b) advanced a quality-ladder theory in which each product innovation is introduced by a new firm, while the firms selling the old products are driven out of business. The concept of a quality ladder refers to a model in which new, higher-quality products affect the value of existing ones.

Caballero and Jaffe (1993) and Klette and Griliches (1997), among others, also delineated a fully specified endogenous growth model, which extends the Grossman and Helpman framework by drawing in elements from the patent, race literature, as discussed in Gilbert and Newberry (1982, 1984) and in Reinganum (1985), and the discrete choice models of product differentiation, as discussed in Anderson *et al.* (1992) and Berry (1994).

Enthusiasm for new growth theory sparked an inevitable backlash for devotees of old growth theory. Specifically, neoclassical economists defended old growth theory by noting that if one extended the Solow (1956) model to include a human capital variable, then the empirical evidence is consistent with neoclassical theory. Following Mankiw *et al.* (1992), equation (2.5) can be expanded to include, along with capital and labor, a stock of human capital in vector X. Lichtenberg's (1992) extension of the Solow model also added a stock of research capital.

Critical to the material of this volume is that these studies that helped to define new growth theory not only endogenized technological change – that is, recognized the role of the entrepreneur in the innovation process and the innovation process in the activities of firms – but also most of them allowed for technological spillovers.

New growth theory also more closely examines the role of infrastructure and government, as discussed by DeLong and Summers (1991), Leyden and Link (1992), and Hall and Jones (1996), as well as a wide range of institutional factors and organizations that influence growth, as discussed by Barro and Sala-i-Martin (1998). Some of these authors also attempt to examine sociological factors as well. Like the earlier stream of growth theory, some of this theoretical work has

Table 3.2 Comparison of old growth theory and new growth theory

Assumptions regarding	Old growth theory	New growth theory
Returns to scale	Constant returns to scale	Increasing returns to scale
Market structure of output and input markets	Perfect competition	Imperfect competition (some models allow for Schumpeterian competition)
Institutional factors influencing growth	Not considered	Considered in some models
Externalities (technological or otherwise)	No externalities	Allows for externalities
Technological change	Exogenous	Endogenous

Early theoretical and empirical studies of economic growth 19

been driven by the availability of a comprehensive data set containing international comparisons of Real National Accounts across countries, constructed by Summers and Heston (1988).

Table 3.2 summarizes the key differences between old growth theory and new growth theory. To summarize, old growth theories typically assumed constant returns to scale, price-taking behavior, an absence of spillovers associated with investment in private capital, and exogenous technological change. These studies also ignored institutional factors and the role of government. New growth theory, in contrast, typically allows for increasing returns to scale, imperfect competition, externalities associated with private investment in physical or technical capital, and endogenous technological change. Some authors also consider institutional factors and the role of government.

4 The production function concept of technological change

Factor-saving classification schemes

One method for evaluating the effect of technological change on production is in terms of changes in the amount of capital (K) and labor (L) used in production, assuming of course that K and L are the only two factors of production. We recognize that intermediate materials and services, and even money, are also utilized in producing goods and services. For expositional purposes, we focus on these two inputs only. The simplest classification scheme assumes that technological change alters the input mix for a given level of output. For a given level of output and input price ratio, a labor-saving technological change results in a higher capital-to-labor ratio; a capital-saving technological change results in a lower capital-to-labor ratio; and a neutral technological change results in an unchanged capital-to-labor ratio.

Consider isoquant I in Figure 4.1, which corresponds to an output level of Q^*. A labor-saving technological change is illustrated as isoquant I shifting inward to point A, where the capital-to-labor ratio is higher than along the ray K/L. Similarly, a capital-saving technological change is illustrated as isoquant I shifting inward to point B where the capital-to-labor ratio is lower than along ray K/L. A neutral technological change results in an inward shift of isoquant I to point C. At point C, Q^* is produced with an unchanged ratio of capital to labor but with proportionally less of each input.

This factor-saving conceptualization of technological change implicitly assumes that technology leads to cost-reducing changes in the production process, rather than to new or improved quality products. Very roughly, this notion highlights the distinction between a process innovation and a product innovation, a subject we will return to in Chapter 9 where we discuss empirical analyses of the impact of R&D on productivity growth.

This factor-saving classification scheme is most applicable at the microeconomic – plant, firm, or industry – level with a focus on the short run when output levels can meaningfully be thought of as remaining constant. The classification scheme represents an unrealistic starting point for a macroeconomic taxonomy when output levels will change.

Alternative factor-saving classification schemes dominate the very early technological change literature and are discussed below. The schemes are based not

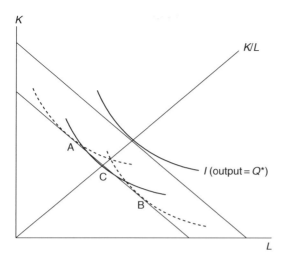

Figure 4.1 Labor-saving, capital-saving, and neutral technological change with output held constant.

on a constant level of output but rather on a constant factor-to-factor or factor-to-output ratio. All of the schemes were set forth within the neoclassical tradition.

As formulated by Hicks (1932), so-called Hicksian technological change is defined as labor-saving, capital-saving, or neutral if the technological change – that is, the adoption of the underlying innovation – raises, lowers, or leaves unchanged the marginal product of capital relative to the marginal product of labor for a given capital-to-labor ratio. Formally, if the production function introduced in equation (2.1) is represented as:

$$Q = f(K, L, t) \tag{4.1}$$

and if the function $f(K, L, t)$ is linearly homogeneous and twice differentiable:

$$f_K, f_L > 0 \quad \text{and} \quad f_{KK}, f_{LL} < 0 \tag{4.2}$$

then, as outlined in Nadiri (1970), it follows that disembodied technological change, or technological change that is independent of factor inputs, is Hicks labor-saving if:

$$\left\{ \frac{\partial [(f_K/K)/(f_L/L)]}{\partial t} \right\}_{K/L \text{ constant}} > 0. \tag{4.3}$$

22 The production function concept of technological change

It is Hicks neutral if:

$$\left\{\frac{\partial[(f_K/K)/(f_L/L)]}{\partial t}\right\}_{K/L \text{ constant}} = 0. \tag{4.4}$$

And, it is Hicks capital-saving if:

$$\left\{\frac{\partial[(f_K/K)/(f_L/L)]}{\partial t}\right\}_{K/L \text{ constant}} < 0. \tag{4.5}$$

Following, for example, Diamond (1965), Fei and Ranis (1965), and Ferguson (1971), the Hicksian scheme can alternatively be specified in terms of a parameter that reflects a Hicksian bias, B. Technological change is Hicks labor-saving if:

$$B = \left\{\left(\frac{\partial f_K/\partial t}{f_K}\right) - \left(\frac{\partial f_L/\partial t}{f_L}\right)\right\} > 0. \tag{4.6}$$

It is Hicks neutral if:

$$B = \left\{\left(\frac{\partial f_K/\partial t}{f_K}\right) - \left(\frac{\partial f_L/\partial t}{f_L}\right)\right\} = 0. \tag{4.7}$$

And, it is Hicks capital-saving if:

$$B = \left\{\left(\frac{\partial f_K/\partial t}{f_K}\right) - \left(\frac{\partial f_L/\partial t}{f_L}\right)\right\} < 0. \tag{4.8}$$

Hicks (1932: 124–5) first introduced the idea that technological bias is inherent within an economic system, noting that a "change in the relative prices of the factors of production is itself a spur to economizing the use of a factor which has become relatively expensive." Salter (1966) disputed this claim by Hicks, asserting that firms seek total cost reduction rather than saving on a single factor, but the endogeniety of factor bias has continued to be stressed in the literature.

Harrod's (1948) classification scheme is similar to that of Hicks, as represented in equations (4.3) through (4.5) except that the capital-to-output ratio is assumed constant rather than the capital-to-labor ratio. Thus, technological change is Harrod labor-saving if:

$$\left\{\frac{\partial[(f_K/K)/(f_L/L)]}{\partial t}\right\}_{K/Q \text{ constant}} > 0. \tag{4.9}$$

It is Harrod neutral if:

$$\left\{\frac{\partial[(f_K/K)/(f_L/L)]}{\partial t}\right\}_{K/Q \text{ constant}} = 0. \tag{4.10}$$

And, it is Harrod capital-saving if:

$$\left\{\frac{\partial[(f_K/K)/(f_L/L)]}{\partial t}\right\}_{K/Q \text{ constant}} < 0. \tag{4.11}$$

Solow's (1967) classification scheme is similar to that of Harrod, as represented in equations (4.9) through (4.11), except that the labor-to-output ratio is assumed constant. Thus, technological change is Solow labor-saving if:

$$\left\{\frac{\partial[(f_K/K)/(f_L/L)]}{\partial t}\right\}_{L/Q \text{ constant}} > 0. \tag{4.12}$$

It is Solow neutral if:

$$\left\{\frac{\partial[(f_K/K)/(f_L/L)]}{\partial t}\right\}_{L/Q \text{ constant}} = 0. \tag{4.13}$$

And, it is Solow capital-saving if:

$$\left\{\frac{\partial[(f_K/K)/(f_L/L)]}{\partial t}\right\}_{L/Q \text{ constant}} < 0. \tag{4.14}$$

Each of these classification schemes – Hicks', Harrod's, and Solow's – is a useful theoretical construct for thinking about the impact of technological change on production, although the Hicksian scheme has dominated the literature. The descriptive usefulness of each is subject to empirical verification.

Production function-based measures of productivity

The aggregate production function

Partial factor productivity and total factor productivity estimates are formulated on the implicit assumption that a production function accurately describes the maximum output attainable from a set of factor inputs. This production process is inherently microeconomic in nature. Questions arise regarding its meaning when

24 The production function concept of technological change

applied at the aggregate level, at which most of the early empirical calculations were made. To illustrate the microeconomic foundations and aggregate shortcomings of a production function, consider a rigorous derivation of the production function from equation (2.5).

To work backwards and derive equation (2.5), one begins with a generalized multi-input and multi-output production function written as:

$$H(Q_{1t}, \ldots, Q_{mt}; X_{1t}, \ldots, X_{nt}; t) = H(\tilde{Q}; \tilde{X}; t) = 0, \qquad (4.15)$$

where the symbol ~ denotes vectors of m-numbered outputs (Qs) and n-numbered inputs (Xs). Following Sudit and Finger (1981), if the function H is homothetic – meaning factor shares are invariant to changes in scale – and weakly separable as defined by H*, then, by definition, one can write:

$$H(\tilde{Q}; \tilde{X}; t) = H^*(G^*(\tilde{Q}); F^*(\tilde{X}); t) = 0 \qquad (4.16)$$

and if the separability of the function is additive, then:

$$G(\tilde{Q}) = F(\tilde{X}; t). \qquad (4.17)$$

Finally, if the multi-output vector is replaced by a single composite output vector, Q, and if time-related technology is Hicks neutral and disembodied, then equation (4.17) becomes:

$$Q = A(t) f(\mathbf{X}), \qquad (4.18)$$

which is identical to equation (2.5).

At the aggregate level the assumption of separability is questionable. Sudit and Finger (1981: 8), for example, contend that the assumption is "economically restrictive since most production processes ... probably do not in general exhibit independence of input and output substitution rates along the efficiency frontiers." Others, such as Afriat (1972), object to the production-function concept in general, regardless of the level of aggregation. They argue that it is inherently impossible to measure the physical efficiency of any production process and that it is unrealistic to believe that firms know all efficient input combinations. Thus, the implicit assumption of production efficiency is unrealistic.

In addition to these concerns, the parameter $A(t)$ is itself a potential source for measurement error. This shift factor reflects only one aspect of the production-related effects of technological change. Being a shift factor, $A(t)$ definitionally does not measure movement along the production function. As a result, following Aigner and Chu (1968) and Nishimizu and Page (1982), any comparison of productivity indices between points in time implicitly assumes either that all inputs – including management – are efficiently utilized at the production surface, or that the extent of inefficiency – input inefficiency or organizational inefficiency – is constant over time.

Nelson and Winter (1982) motivate their evolutionary model of growth in part on the basis of their dissatisfaction with certain alleged shortcomings in the neoclassical model. In the view of these authors, the neoclassical model allows no room for purposive entrepreneurial activity or innovational search in the production process. In the neoclassical tradition, technical knowledge is a pure public good – firms can select in a profit maximizing way from all known technical possibilities to produce their output, whether the technical possibilities have been tried or not. Nothing is assumed to be unknown. Although Nelson and Winter's evolutionary model does not offer an alternative to total factor productivity measurement – in fact, they define it away – they do offer an important framework for questioning the logic behind approximating technological change simply by changes in a time-related shift factor.

The above criticisms about the production function framework are not without merit. Still, apart from data problems, the production-function approach appears to have considerable construct validity. According to Nadiri (1970: 1146):

> [T]he use of an aggregate production function gives reasonably good estimates... due mainly to the narrow range of movement of aggregate data rather than the solid foundation of the function.

The aggregate production continues to perform well in econometric estimation, as evidenced by Mankiw *et al.* (1992) and Lichtenberg (1992).

Partial factor productivity indices

Labor productivity indices, the most commonly used partial factor productivity measures, have been popular in the academic and policy literatures for decades partly because of their ease of calculation.

Academics have been especially frustrated at the difficulty in constructing accurate measures of capital input, which would be used in constructing estimates of a capital productivity index as well as a total factor productivity index. Therefore, many have resigned themselves to the analysis of labor productivity. McGuckin and Nguyen (1995), Foster *et al.* (1998), and Disney *et al.* (2000), along with many others, make inferences about overall economic efficiency based on labor productivity indices.

However, this analytical advantage, or short cut, is not without its cost. For example, the use of Q/L, or the average product of labor, as a measure of productivity has, according to Perloff and Wachter (1980: 116), "numerous serious, if not quite fatal conceptual flaws." Even so, labor productivity indices still remain widely used. According to Christiansen and Haveman (1980: 3), "although [these] productivity measures... have serious weaknesses, the picture of productivity change which they yield is not greatly different from that of more complete measures." Three of the flaws associated with labor productivity measures are discussed below.

First, to ensure reliability, output and input measures must be consistent, that is, they must refer to the same production activity. Since there are many production activities implicitly underlying any aggregate measure of output, a meaningful composite measure must be formulated by denominating the value of each output measure by an appropriate prices index. However, when labor is denominated in hours, conceptual problems arise because a labor-hours measure corrects for only one of the many heterogeneous aspects of workers, namely and obviously the number of hours each works. Additional adjustments are needed. For example, the age/sex/skill composition of the labor force varies over time as well as from sector to sector. Since average labor productivity indices are primarily used for intertemporal comparisons, changes in the composition of the workforce will affect measured Q, but will not be reflected accurately in a Q/L index unless the changes are perfectly correlated with the way in which L is measured. This conceptual problem can be overcome by adjusting L for the heterogeneity of the labor force and thereby creating an index with efficiency labor units in the denominator.

Siegel (1997) describes one method for constructing such an index based on methods used by the US Bureau of Labor Statistics (BLS) and based on their data. Following Chinloy (1980), Siegel's index is calculated on the basis of changes in both the number of hours worked and hourly wages earned by different types of workers, classified by age and education level. Similar indexes of labor productivity or quality have been used by others, such as, for example, Jorgenson et al. (1987) and Dean et al. (1988) in studies of aggregate economic growth. It is important to note that these indexes are also based on the assumption that labor markets are perfectly competitive, as noted in Chinloy (1980).

Chinloy (1980) defines labor quality, LQ, changes as:

$$(\partial \ln LQ_t/\partial t) = \sum_i (v_{it} - b_{it}) (\partial \ln h_{it}/\partial t), \qquad (4.19)$$

where h_{it} is hours worked by the ith type of labor in year t, v_{it} is the share of total compensation paid to the ith type of labor, and $\{b_{it} = (h_{it}/m_t)\}$ is the share of total hours worked devoted to the ith labor type. The discrete approximation for equation (4.19) is:

$$QUALIND_t = \sum_i \tfrac{1}{2} (v_{it} + v_{i,t-1}) (\ln h_{it} + \ln h_{i,t-1})$$
$$- (\ln m_t - \ln m_{t-1}), \qquad (4.20)$$

where $QUALIND_t$ is a quality index that approximates the left-hand-side of equation (4.19). In constructing these indexes, the key data requirements are a set of employment attributes to identify each of the i different types of labor.

There are several ways to aggregate over the heterogeneous outputs that are generally used in either partial factor-productivity or total factor-productivity indices. The base-year approach adjusts output values by the price of each product in the base year. The deflated-price approach adjusts the value of each product by a current average price index. The choice between the two approaches is important. According to Baumol and Wolff (1984), the base-year measure is a defensible index for productivity growth comparisons. However, the authors point out that it is not a useful indicator of interindustry or intersectoral differences in absolute levels of productivity. Similarly, the deflated price index is meaningful for intra-industry comparisons of absolute levels of productivity over time, but it too fails to provide meaningful cross-sectional comparisons. The search for a valid cross-sectional index of absolute production still continues.

A second problem with labor productivity measures is that the average product of labor could be related to the business cycle, and thus could suggest trends that are unrelated to technical progress. Indeed, Gordon (1979), for example, contended that firms retain more workers in the last stage of a business cycle than is justified *ex post* by the future level of output. As a result of such biased *ex ante* expectations, Q/L will decline absolutely until firms adjust their hiring patterns to their corrected expectations about future demand.

A third and perhaps, the most serious concern regarding labor productivity measures is that neither labor nor capital is the sole source of productivity improvements. Labor-saving improvement resulting from other factors of production are improperly attributed as an improvement in labor productivity when these other factors are not held constant. That is, a major problem with the use of labor productivity as a metric for economic performance is that it measures the efficiency of only one input and does not control for the possibility that the plant, firm, or industry can substitute capital, materials, or services for labor. Many shun partial factor-productivity indices precisely for this reason. A useful and meaningful productivity framework must therefore identify the source of the productivity improvement and their interaction with other factors of production, such as capital, materials, and services in the overall production process. Along similar lines, Craig and Harris (1973) showed that partial factor-productivity measures do not quantify the impact of technical substitution. If, for example, a new technology is embodied in capital, Q/L could rise as a result of capital for labor substitution, *ceteris paribus*. But if the cost of the new capital-embodied technology equals the cost savings from fewer workers, then total production costs are unchanged and the initial movement in Q/L is misleading with regard to actual productivity gains.

Total factor productivity indices

Solow's (1957) pioneering study was the first to posit explicitly an aggregate production function. His Divisia or geometric index was formulated from a Cobb–Douglas production function written in terms of capital and labor, and was characterized by linear homogeneity and disembodied Hicks neutral technological change. The functional form that Solow worked from was:

$$Q = A(t)K^\alpha L^\beta, \tag{4.21}$$

where, assuming perfect competition and constant returns to scale, and where, α and β ($\alpha + \beta = 1$) are the shares of income distributed to capital and labor respectively. From equation (4.21), it follows that the impact of technological change on production can be approximated as a residual growth rate. Taking the natural logarithm of both sides of equation (4.21) yields:

$$\ln Q = \ln A(t) + \alpha \ln K + \beta \ln L \qquad (4.22)$$

Taking the time derivative of both sides of equation (4.22) and rearranging terms yields, with reference to equation (2.6):

$$\left\{\frac{\partial \ln A/\partial t}{\ln A}\right\} = \left\{\frac{\partial \ln Q/\partial t}{\ln Q}\right\} - \alpha\left\{\frac{\partial \ln K/\partial t}{\ln K}\right\} - \beta\left\{\frac{\partial \ln L/\partial t}{\ln L}\right\} \qquad (4.23)$$

or, redefining the left-hand-side of equation (4.23) and using equation (2.8):

$$\left\{\frac{\partial TFP/\partial t}{TFP}\right\} = \left\{\frac{\partial A/\partial t}{A}\right\} = A'/A. \qquad (4.24)$$

More descriptively, technological change, denoted in equation (4.24) as A'/A, represents the percentage change in output per year that is not explained by the annual percentage change in capital and labor. In other words, A'/A is an impact indicator. As Domar (1961: 712) more realistically characterized the results of this model, "A is a residual. It absorbs, like a sponge, all increases in output not accounted for by the growth of explicitly recognized inputs." Certainly, if the underlying production function was specified in terms of several inputs, A could mathematically be constructed given each input's relative share, but the interpretation of such a constructed measure would remain the same – a residual.

This Solow residual measure of total factor-productivity growth has formed the foundation for an extensive body of empirical literature, part of which includes studies attempting to correlate investments in technology with A'/A. However, despite its widespread use, the index does not distinguish between pure technological change and changes in efficiency with which properly measured resources, including technology, are used. This shortcoming has motivated many to move to a frontier production-function framework, as described in Appendix B. Other shortcomings of the Solow residual are that it picks up the effects of sub-optimal capacity utilization, returns to scale, mismeasurement of inputs and output, and imperfect competition.

The Cobb–Douglas production function in equation (4.21) has several unique features. Technological change is simultaneously Hicks neutral, Harrod neutral, and Solow neutral. If $A(t) = e^{\lambda t}$ in equation (4.21), with λ being a parameter reflecting the rate of disembodied technological change, then, following Stoneman (1983), technological change is Hicks neutral at rate m:

$$Q = e^{mt} K^\alpha L^{1-\alpha} = (Ke^{mt})^\alpha (Le^{mt})^{1-\alpha}; \quad \lambda = m \qquad (4.25)$$

and Harrod neutral at rate m:

$$Q = e^{m(1-\alpha)t} K^\alpha L^{1-\alpha} = K^\alpha (Le^{mt})^{1-\alpha}; \quad \lambda = m(1-\alpha) \tag{4.26}$$

and Solow neutral at rate m:

$$Q = e^{m\alpha t} K^\alpha L^{1-\alpha} = (Ke^{mt})^\alpha L^{1-\alpha}; \quad \lambda = m\alpha. \tag{4.27}$$

The explicit assumption of neutrality is a limitation associated with any total factor productivity index derived from a Cobb–Douglas specification. There is some empirical evidence that technical progress has been labor-saving over time, as was originally hypothesized by Hicks (1932). The pioneering work in this regard traces to Moroney (1972), Binswanger (1974) and Binswanger and Ruttan (1978), and Cain and Patterson (1981). Moroney (1972) found strong evidence from 1949 to 1962 that technological change was not Hicks neutral with US manufacturing industries. In 11 of 20 two-digit SIC industries studies, the bias was labor-saving. Cain and Patterson (1981) reached a similar finding using historical US manufacturing data over the period 1850 to 1919. Binswanger (1974) and Binswanger and Ruttan (1978) reported that technological changes in US agriculture between 1912 and 1968 were biased. These changes were fertilizer-using and labor-saving, accompanied by a decrease and increase respectively in those factors' prices. Subsequent research, using microeconomic data sets and more advanced econometric techniques, validates these foundation conclusions.

The Cobb–Douglas specification also implies that the elasticity of substitution, σ, is unity. This is thought by some to be a troublesome assumption because it fails to measure productivity gains, which may result from changes that permit more flexible substitution of inputs in the production process. For example, consider a generalized two-input production function that allows for non-neutral technical progress as:

$$Q = F(K, L, t) = G(a(t)K, b(t)L). \tag{4.28}$$

From this more general specification, Hicks neutrality implies that $a(t) = b(t)$, that is, technological change is equally capital- and labor-augmenting. Harrod neutrality implies that $a(t) = 1$, meaning that technological change is labor-augmenting. Finally, Solow neutrality implies that $b(t) = 1$, meaning that technological change is capital-augmenting.

The constant elasticity of substitution (CES) production function, originated by Arrow et al. (1961) and reviewed by Nerlove (1967), is a production function that exhibits pure factor augmentation:

$$Q = \{(a(t)K)^{-\rho} + (b(t)L)^{-\rho}\}^{-1/\rho}, \tag{4.29}$$

where the elasticity of substitution is:

$$\sigma = 1/(1+\rho). \tag{4.30}$$

Following David and van de Klundert (1965), Hicksian bias, B, is:

$$B = \left\{ \frac{\partial a(t)/\partial t}{a(t)} - \frac{\partial b(t)/\partial t}{b(t)} \right\} \left(1 - \frac{1}{\sigma}\right). \tag{4.31}$$

Technical progress, as suggested by equation (4.31), is not independent of σ. Technical progress is labor-saving as:

$$\sigma > 1 \quad \text{and} \quad \left\{ \frac{\partial a(t)/\partial t}{a(t)} > \frac{\partial b(t)/\partial t}{b(t)} \right\} \tag{4.32}$$

or

$$\sigma < 1 \quad \text{and} \quad \left\{ \frac{\partial a(t)/\partial t}{a(t)} < \frac{\partial b(t)/\partial t}{b(t)} \right\}. \tag{4.33}$$

Technical progress is capital-saving if:

$$\sigma > 1 \quad \text{and} \quad \left\{ \frac{\partial b(t)/\partial t}{b(t)} > \frac{\partial a(t)/\partial t}{a(t)} \right\} \tag{4.34}$$

or

$$\sigma < 1 \quad \text{and} \quad \left\{ \frac{\partial b(t)/\partial t}{b(t)} < \frac{\partial a(t)/\partial t}{a(t)} \right\}. \tag{4.35}$$

Kalt (1978), early on, simultaneously estimated the rate of capital- and labor-augmenting technological change and the elasticity of substitution for the US private domestic economy from 1929 to 1967. Using a CES production-function specification, the estimated elasticity of substitution was 0.76. The rate of capital-augmenting technological change was estimated to be near zero.

Nelson (1965) showed that there is little difference between results obtained when estimating productivity growth using the CES and the Cobb–Douglas specifications. Rates of technical progress for the US economy based on a CES specification are very similar to the Solow Cobb–Douglas estimates.

Kendrick's (1956) discrete arithmetic index of productivity change is consistent with a CES production function. His discrete index is:

$$\frac{\Delta A}{A} = \left\{ \frac{Q_1/Q_0}{(wL_1 + rK_1)/(wL_0 + rK_0)} \right\} - 1. \tag{4.36}$$

where w is the wage rate, r is the rate of return on capital or rental price of capital, and the numerical subscripts refer to discrete time periods, with 0 being the initial time period.

Constant returns to scale is an assumption frequently made when estimating a Cobb–Douglas and CES production function, as noted above. With reference to the Cobb–Douglas production function in equation (4.21), this implies that $(\alpha + \beta) = 1$. With reference to the CES production function in equation (4.29), variable returns to scale are represented by the exponent $(-v/\rho)$, where v is the scale parameter and when $v = 1$ constant returns to scale are explicit, as in equation (4.29). The assumption of constant returns to scale, while mathematically appealing, distorts the meaning of total factor productivity indices derived from equation (4.36) because no distinction can be made between pure Hicksian neutral technical progress and efficiencies resulting from an increasing realization of scale economies. Sato (1980) showed theoretically that such ambiguity could only be removed by estimating a non-homothetic production function for a given type of technical progress. A production function is holothetic under a given type of technical progress if the scale effect and the technology effects are indistinguishable.

Walters (1963) was the first to re-estimate Solow's (1957) aggregate production function using the 1909 to 1949 aggregate data for the US economy. He provided strong evidence suggesting that what was originally viewed by Solow as neutral technological change may have actually been growth due to production efficiencies resulting from economies of scale. Walters' estimates of annual technical progress are about one-third smaller than Solow's. Of course, his estimates do not account for the interaction between technology and scale economies: as new technology embodied in capital enters production, the potential economies from an increase in scale also increase.

Finally, any total factor productivity indices that do not explicitly account for intermediate inputs, when constructing the denominator expression, or for the potential of factor substitution between intermediate inputs and capital or labor, are inherently biased. At the microeconomic level, the value of intermediate goods and services should be subtracted from gross output, leaving some measure of real value added to approximate Q. So doing implicitly assumes that the underlying production function is additively separable in the form $Q = f(VA + M)$, where VA represents value added and M represents intermediate inputs. If total productivity indices are to be reliable estimators, intermediate inputs must be accounted for on the input side.

Researchers have not only measured technical progress residually through a total factor productivity index, but they have also taken more explicit steps to account for the accuracy of input measures. Specifically, care has been taken to weight the components of labor and capital inputs properly, as suggested by equation (2.7), to account more accurately for heterogeneous quality differences. Once done, the relative importance of real input growth for real output growth increases quantitatively.

The early theoretical work in this regard, from the 1950s, focuses on the heterogeneity of capital. Realizing that new and more productive technologies can be embodied in successive vintages of capital, rather than simply augmenting a homogeneous stock of capital, Johansen (1959) and Solow (1960) conceptualized the following Cobb–Douglas vintage production function:

$$Q_v(t) = B(v)K_v(t)^\alpha L_v(t)^{1-\alpha}, \tag{4.37}$$

32 *The production function concept of technological change*

where $Q_v(t)$ represents output produced at time t using capital of vintage v, $B(v)$ is a vintage-specific disembodied shift parameter, $K_v(t)$ is the stock of capital from vintage v in operation at period t, and $L_v(t)$ is the labor used with vintage v capital at period t. Also at time t, the technology-adjusted capital stock, $J(t)$, is:

$$J(t) = \int_{-\infty}^{t} B(v)K_v(t)\, dv. \tag{4.38}$$

There have been numerous empirical applications of the vintage model, beginning with Solow (1960, 1962), using aggregate data for the US economy. Each study, however, failed to provide strong support for the vintage specification. Although, making vintage adjustments did reduce the size of A'/A, the size of the adjustment was small. According to Nelson (1964: 590), commenting about the vintage approach having demonstrated empirically that the embodiment effect is small:

> Somehow many economists have come to view the requirement that new technology be embodied in new capital as in some sense a happy phenomenon. The reason for this seems to lie in the greater sensitivity of the growth rate to the investment rate that embodiment implies. But surely, the less the requirements for new technology to be embodied in new capital, the less costly is faster growth. Of course it might be replied that if growth itself were an objective regardless of cost, and if it were easier to influence $\Delta K/K$ than other variables that affect growth, then a strong embodiment provides a strong handle for policy. But surely this is a strange argument.

Greater empirical support for vintage models has come from cross-industry studies, especially studies of the electric-power industry. However, one could argue that a portion of vintage adjustments is really a control for the quality heterogeneity of capital.

Second-generation efforts at estimating technological change from a production-function perspective have not only adjusted all relevant inputs for quality but also have experimented with alternative functional forms. Christensen *et al.* (1971, 1973) advanced the state of the art by more accurately capturing the effect of scale economies and input substitution on a measure of technological change. Beginning with the general representation:

$$Q = F(K, L, t) \tag{4.39}$$

technological change is indexed, under the assumption of constant returns to scale, as:

$$v_t = \frac{\partial Q/\partial t}{Q} - v_K \left\{ \frac{\partial Q/\partial t}{K} \right\} - v_L \left\{ \frac{\partial Q/\partial t}{L} \right\} \tag{4.40}$$

where, following their notation, v_K and v_L are the distributive shares of capital and labor in the value of output. Previously, we have represented these shares as α and β.

More specifically, when F(K, L, t) is specified as a transcendental logarithmic or translog function:

$$Q = \exp \{ \alpha_0 + \alpha_L \ln L + \alpha_K \ln K + \alpha_t t \\
+ \tfrac{1}{2} (\beta_{KK} (\ln K)^2) + \beta_{KL} \ln K \ln L \\
+ \beta_{Kt} (t) \ln K + \tfrac{1}{2} (\beta_{LL} (\ln L)^2) \\
+ \beta_{Lt} (t) \ln L + \tfrac{1}{2} (\beta_{tt} t^2) \}. \tag{4.41}$$

While many researchers have employed such a model, the insights from the initial Christensen et al. (1980) effort are especially relevant. They compared aggregate growth patterns among the United States, Canada, France, Germany, Italy, Japan, Korea, the Netherlands, and the United Kingdom between 1960 and 1973 and for selected earlier periods. They concluded that (1) cross-country variations in real product growth were associated with the growth of real factor inputs, a conclusion, if isolated, that could have been arrived at using simpler production functions; and (2) any analysis that failed to incorporate quality changes in input measures will overstate the contribution of total factor productivity growth to the growth of real product.

At a microeconomic level, Gollop and Roberts (1981: 173) examined 1948 to 1973 data from the US manufacturing sector and concluded that an indirect, as well as direct, contribution by inputs to the rate of technological change exists: "The indirect effect on technical change is a function of substitution possibilities and the factor-using/factor-saving nature of technical change." Along similar lines, Fraumeni and Jorgenson (1981) determined that capital formation was the most important source of the growth in aggregate value added between 1948 and 1976. Also, the influence of reallocated capital between sectors in the economy on changes in total factor productivity was found to be minimal.

While the above discussion is grounded in a production-function framework, duality theory has afforded many researchers the ability to estimate technological change based on a cost-function framework. We retain the production-function framework through this volume.

5 Alternative frameworks for measuring technical progress and productivity

Growth accounting

Any residually measured total factor productivity index confounds the productivity gains achieved from better inputs and greater organizational efficiency – movement toward the production function – with the output from process-related technological change. Of course, what may be classified as organizational or management efficiency in one firm or one industry could result from a technological breakthrough or an entrepreneurial insight in another firm or another industry. This relationship suggests the importance of technology diffusion on the measured productivity growth of any one firm or industry. Some do not view this as an issue at the aggregate level, except in the case of international technology transfer. However, it is an issue in the sense that the diffusion of technology supports new growth theory by emphasizing purposive actions in the identification, adoption, and implementation of others' technology, that is, technological change is endogenous.

Beginning with Denison (1962), efforts were made to identify empirically factors underlying changes in a production-function shift parameter or index such as $A(t)$. That is, economists were not simply interested in measuring the productivity residual, but also explaining it. Once the key explanatory factors could be identified, policies could be formulated to enhance economic growth. The first order of business was to make sure that the researcher had actually measured technological change correctly.

In analytical terms, growth accounting is an attempt to remove from the $A(t)$ residual all factors except a pure technological-change component. The idea being, of course, that by breaking down observable output growth into components associated with measurable factor inputs, a purer residual will result, and that residual will represent or measure technological change. After Denison's pioneering research, he and others pursued to decompose total factor productivity growth into a number of categories. This early research of Denison (1967, 1972, 1974, 1979, 1984), Kendrick (1973), and Jorgenson and Griliches (1967), and others, is summarized in terms of the more recent work of Kendrick and Grossman (1980) as reported in Table 5.1. The average annual growth rate of total factor productivity in the US domestic economy between 1966 and 1976 was 1.4 percent. In that time period, advances in knowledge – for example, from R&D, learning by

Table 5.1 Growth accounting components of growth in real gross US product: 1948–66 and 1966–76 (in percentage points)

Components	1948–66	1966–76
Growth per annum in:		
Real gross product	3.9	2.8
Tangible factor inputs	1.0	1.4
Total factor productivity	2.9	1.4
Advances in knowledge	1.4	1.1
Changes in labor quality	0.6	0.5
Changes in land quality	0.0	−0.1
Resource reallocations	0.3	0.1
Volume-related factors	0.6	−0.2
Government activity	0.0	−0.1
Residual	0.0	0.1

Source: Kendrick and Grossman (1980).

doing and related experiences – were estimated as accounting for 1.1 percentage points of the 1.4 percent increase; changes in labor quality – for example, changes in education, health, and the age/sex/skill composition of the work force – was estimated as accounting for 0.5 percentage points; changes in the quality of land for −0.1 percentage points; resource reallocations – for example, inter-industry labor shifts – for 0.1 percentage points; volume-related factors, such as economies of scale and intensity of demand, for −0.2 percentage points; and government regulations for −0.1 percentage points. The residual in Table 5.1, or more accurately the residual of the residual, or the not elsewhere classified component of growth, accounted for 0.1 percentage points of the 1.4 percentage rate of growth.

Jorgenson and Griliches (1967) were able to fully explain the residual $A(t)$ by adjusting inputs for quality and more accurately accounting for aggregation biases. This was an important effort because their empirical analysis carefully demonstrated that Solow (1957) had greatly overestimated the contribution made by technological change to the productivity growth of the first half of the twentieth century. A second important finding of Jorgenson and Griliches (1967) was their demonstration that one could construct a dual measure of the Solow residual, which is derived mathematically from the equality of output (Q) and factor incomes:

$$Q = p_K K + p_L L, \tag{5.1}$$

where p_K is the rental price of capital which was denoted by r in Chapter 4, and p_L is the wage or price of labor which was denoted by w in Chapter 4. Computing time derivatives on both sides of equation (5.1), dividing by Q, and rearranging terms, much in the same fashion as in the Solow (1957) analysis, yields:

$$\frac{\partial Q/\partial t}{Q} = \left\{ s_K \left(\frac{\partial p_K/\partial t}{p_K} + \frac{\partial K/\partial t}{K} \right) \right\} + \left\{ s_L \left(\frac{\partial p_L/\partial t}{p_L} + \frac{\partial L/\partial t}{L} \right) \right\}, \tag{5.2}$$

where s_K and s_L – α and β from equation (4.21) – are the factor shares of capital and labor, respectively. Jorgenson and Griliches showed that if terms were rearranged, the dual of the growth of total factor productivity (TFP) could be expressed as:

$$\frac{\partial TFP/\partial t}{TFP} = \frac{Q'}{Q} - s_K \frac{K'}{K} - s_L \frac{L'}{L} = \frac{s_K p_K'}{p_K} + \frac{s_L p_L'}{p_L}, \quad (5.3)$$

where

$$Q'/Q = \{(\partial Q/\partial t) / Q\} \quad (5.4)$$
$$K'/K = \{(\partial K/\partial t) / K\} \quad (5.5)$$
$$L'/L = \{(\partial L/\partial t) / L\} \quad (5.6)$$
$$p_K'/p_K = \{(\partial p_K/\partial t) / p_K\} \quad (5.7)$$
$$p_L'/p_L = \{(\partial p_L/\partial t) / p_L\}. \quad (5.8)$$

Note that the dual measure of TFP growth uses the same factor shares as the production function based measure of TFP growth developed in Chapter 4; however, in the dual, TFP growth is based on changes in input prices – p_K and p_L – instead of input quantities – K and L.

One of the lessons learned from these early growth accounting studies is that carefully measured inputs are critical to the development of meaningful productivity indices. As well, these early studies highlighted the importance of technological change as an aggregate force driving productivity growth, and thus economic performance. Partly as a result of the findings of the early growth accounting studies, researchers began to focus on the microeconomic determinants of technological change, R&D activity in particular. This point is reemphasized in Chapter 9. The emphasis by researchers on investments in knowledge through R&D set the stage for policy makers, especially those in the United States, in the late 1970s and early 1980s to similarly focus on R&D as a target variable.

A resurgence in interest and application of growth-accounting techniques occurred in the late 1980s and early- to mid-1990s as researchers attempted to quantify the impact of information technology (IT) on economic growth. Sichel (1997), Jorgenson and Stiroh (1995), and Oliner and Sichel (1997), relied on growth-accounting frameworks to analyze the impact of IT on aggregate US economic growth in the 1980s, which turned out to be surprisingly quite small. These authors used data from the US Bureau of Economic Analysis (BEA), which disaggregated physical capital into computer capital and non-computer capital. Thus, they could accurately estimate the impact of computer capital on aggregate economic performance. Each of these studies reports that computers have made only a very small contribution to economic growth. This issue is discussed in greater detail in Chapter 10 with reference to the relationship between investment in computers and economic performance.

Output indicators

An alternative to total factor productivity measurement is to assess the direct output resulting from the search for technical knowledge. This approach overcomes some of the difficulties associated with production-function indicators of technical progress, yet it also has problems.

Patents are often used as an indicator of technology output. Such indices are more directly linked to innovative activity rather than to technological change. Although frequently used, there are many well-known problems with patent data. First, few results from scientific inquiry are patentable. Most patents are the result of R&D activity. Researchers, beginning with Scherer (1965a), have shown that there is a strong positive correlation between R&D expenditures and patenting at various levels of aggregation – the firm or the industry – although the evidence is weak that patenting is requisite to appropriating returns to R&D. See Table 5.2 for selected studies about the relationship between R&D expenditures and patent activity.

Second, and more importantly, the propensity to patent depends on corporate policy, which in turn is influenced by the rate and direction of the underlying technology. These two points are not to be interpreted to mean that patenting, and hence patent policy, does not affect inventive and innovative behavior. Patent rights do confer value, as Lanjouw *et al.* (1998) and Schankerman (1998) have shown.

Table 5.2 Selected studies examining the relationship between R&D expenditures and patent activity

Author	Findings
Scherer (1965a)	Calculated the elasticity of patenting with respect to R&D employment as near unity, based on a study of *Fortune* 500 firms in 1955
Schmookler (1966)	Using 1953 data for selected manufacturing industries, determined that large firms spend more than twice as much R&D per patent than small firms
Bound *et al.* (1984)	Verified Scherer's (1965a) elasticity of patenting with respect to R&D of unity using a 1976 cross-section of firms
Hall *et al.* (1986)	Concluded from a study of manufacturing firms that, based on activity from the 1970s, patents are not the only measure of the output of R&D, and the fraction of R&D output represented by patents varies across industry and over time; there is a positive and contemporaneous relationship between patenting and R&D and lagged historical R&D has little relationship to current patenting behavior
Acs and Audretsch (1989)	Demonstrated at the US industry level that patents are a reliable proxy for innovative activity in the late 1970s, and patenting activity is positively related to the level of R&D

Table 5.3 Selected findings using patents as an output indicator

Finding	Author
Strong positive correlation between R&D expenditure (or employment) and patents	Scherer (1965a) Schmookler (1966) Scherer (1983a) Bound et al. (1984) Pakes and Griliches (1984) Hall et al. (1986) Acs and Audretsch (1989)
Positive correlation between patents and market value (stock market rate of return and Tobin's q)	Griliches (1981) Connolly and Hirschey (1982) Ben-Zion (1984) Pakes (1985) Cockburn and Griliches (1988) Austin (1993)
Value of patents is highly skewed, where value is determined by citations	Trajtenberg (1990a) Jaffe et al. (1993) Henderson et al. (1998) Jaffe et al. (1998)
Citation-weighted measures of patents are more highly correlated with market value than unweighted measures	Hall et al. (2000)

Also, patents are an important predictor of activities related to the transfer of knowledge, and knowledge is certainly a determinant of technological change. Link and Scott (2002a) showed that patterns of technology flows that result from licensing agreements among US chemical firms could be predicted on the basis of patent citations. Specifically, Link and Scott demonstrated, among their other findings, that firms with patented technology that is useful to other firms are more likely to have licensing agreements with those other firms.

Other patent-related studies are summarized in Table 5.3.

An alternative output indicator of the success from an innovation process that has been widely used is a count or chronology of major innovations over time. Beginning with the Myers and Marquis (1969) study, others have documented technological success through marketable innovations and have quantified the diffusion of such innovations over time and across industrial uses. They have then associated aspects of technology diffusion with the economic performance. According to Mansfield (1961: 763): "To understand how economic growth is generated, we must know more about the way innovations occur and how they become generally accepted."

Following Geroski (2000), the workhorse diffusion or logistic function model in the economics literature is:

$$y(t) = N\{1 + \varphi \exp(-\kappa t)\}^{-1}, \tag{5.9}$$

Table 5.4 Selected studies of the diffusion of technology

Author	Finding
Griliches (1957)	The adoption of hybrid corn seed from the mid-1930s to mid-1950s within US states over time can be characterized by a logistic curve; cross-state difference in the rate of adoption can be explained in terms of the profitability of adoptions
Mansfield (1961)	The logistically estimated rate at which firms imitate an innovation is explained in terms of the profitability of the innovation and in terms of the population of firms already using the innovation, based on an analysis of 12 innovations over selected years within the 1890–1958 period
Mansfield (1963)	The length of time a firm waits before using a new technique is inversely related to its size and the profitability of investing in the innovation, based on historical data on 14 innovations
Romeo (1975)	Inter-industry (10 US manufacturing industries) differences in the rate at which numerically controlled machine tools replaced conventional machine tools is explained in terms of the amount of R&D done in an industry
Romeo (1977)	Following on Romeo (1975), competitive pressures in an industry also lead to higher rates of diffusion of numerically controlled machine tools
Link and Kapur (1994)	Compatibility and interface standards being in place is critical to the rate of diffusion of flexible manufacturing technology in tooling and machining companies

where $\kappa \equiv \beta N$ and $\varphi \equiv \{(N - y(0))/y(0)\}$, and where β is the probability that each existing user of the technology contacts a non-user. Early studies – such as those by Griliches (1957), Mansfield (1961, 1963), Romeo (1975, 1977) and Link and Kapur (1994) – employed the model in equation (5.1) to focus on modeling the determinants of β. See Table 5.4 for a summary of these authors' findings.

More recently, Link and Scott (2002*b*) broadened the traditional focus of diffusion models, which embraced the concept of an innovation as being a tangible technology, to consider the diffusion of technology-based institutions. Their focus was on science parks. Specifically, Link and Scott implement a Gompertz diffusion model to characterize an organization adopting the innovation of locating in a science park. They let $F(t)$ represent the probability of the location of a particular organization in a science park having occurred at time, t, as:

$$F(t) = 1 - S(t), \tag{5.10}$$

where $S(t)$ is the probability that, for a particular adopter, the adoption has not occurred by time t:

$$S(t) = e \exp(-e^\lambda / \gamma)(e^{\gamma t} - 1). \tag{5.11}$$

Deriving the hazard rate for the model explains the descriptive roles for the two parameters of the model, λ and γ. The hazard rate, $h(t)$, for the adoption is:

$$h(t) = F'(t)/(1 - F(t)), \qquad (5.12)$$

where

$$F'(t) = -S'(t) = e \exp(\lambda + \gamma t) - (e^{\lambda}/\gamma)(e^{\gamma t} - 1). \qquad (5.13)$$

Substituting equations (5.10), (5.11), and (5.13) into equation (5.12), the hazard rate for adoption is thus:

$$h(t) = e^{(\lambda + \gamma t)} + e^{\lambda} e^{\gamma t} \qquad (5.14)$$

and the hazard rate is increasing, decreasing, or constant as γ is $>$, $<$, or $= 0$. Link and Scott apply this diffusion model to a case study of organizations choosing to locate in Research Triangle Park, North Carolina.

Yet another output indicator frequently used is one that directly quantifies the impact of a technology on the affected system, or as Sahal (1981, 1985) refers to as a systems concept of technology. His approach is based on the maintained assumption that a production process is characterized not by a smooth production isoquant but by limited input substitution possibilities. There are generic efficiency characteristics – such as motor horsepower, jet-engine thrust, and computer operations per second – within any production operating system. Thus, changes in system characteristics over time proxies the output of a new technology.

Output indicators may be relatively more useful for measuring technical progress at a microeconomic rather than macroeconomic level, holding institutional characteristics constant, since this methodology does not lend itself well to aggregate generalizations about technologies in general.

Other frameworks

Other imaginative and useful approaches to measuring technical progress employ either an input–output or a management decision framework. Leontief-like (1953) productivity measures are formulated from sectoral input–output models. These models begin with a linear functional relationship, such as following Dogramaci (1981):

$$x_{ij} = \alpha_{ij} X_i / A_i A_j, \qquad (5.15)$$

where x_{ij} is the output of sector j consumed by sector i, the αs are the input coefficients, and the X_i is the net output of sector i. Productivity gains are measured in terms of A_i and A_j. For example, if A_i increases, fewer inputs – that is, outputs from sector j consumed in sector i – are needed in sector i to produce a unit of output X_i. Pioneering researchers to use this approach are Carter (1970) and

Almon (1975) for the US economy. Raa and Wolff (2001) used these techniques to assess the impact of outsourcing on the acceleration of total factor productivity growth in US manufacturing industries.

A number of other approaches to measuring productivity have been suggested by, for example, Gold (1955) and Farrell (1957). Each proffered methods to measure production efficiency in terms of inputs and staged-output ratios, but, as Eilon and Soesan (1976) emphasized, none focuses explicitly on the technology-to-productivity relationship.

6 Trends in productivity growth

International experiences

As discussed in previous chapters, there are several ways to measure productivity growth. Partial factor productivity indices and total factor productivity indices are the most commonly used measures. Both have their merits, as well as their shortfalls.

Two measurement issues are important when comparing productivity growth, assuming of course that inputs and output are correctly measured. First, cross-country comparisons assume that the same production function characterizes the industries in both countries. This assumption is somewhat less troublesome when comparing productivity among developed countries than when making comparisons between developed and undeveloped countries. Second, indices must be standardized for differences in the value of output between countries. However, the common practice of using exchange rates to convert the net output from one country to the currency of the other produces inaccurate estimates because exchange rates proxy relative purchasing power poorly. Therefore, cross-country comparisons so adjusted should be interpreted only as approximating of actual differences in productivity levels.

The data in Table 6.1 show decreases in the average rate of productivity growth in labor, capital, and total factor productivity in selected countries between the 1960–73 and 1973–9 time periods. Labor and total factor productivity growth between 1960 and 1973 was greatest in Japan, although the rates for Italy are nearly as large. Growth rates in Japan were, during that time period, larger than in the United States by more than a factor of three. Between 1973 and 1979, the highest rates of labor and total factor-productivity growth were not in Japan, but in Belgium, West Germany, and France. In each of the nine countries shown in the table, labor, capital, and total factor productivity growth rates were lower in the 1973–9 period than in the 1960–73 period; capital productivity growth was in fact negative in every country between 1973 and 1979.

More detailed international data on total factor productivity are presented in Table 6.2 for earlier and related time periods. These findings suggest that there was a decline in total factor productivity growth in all of the countries listed in the table beginning around 1973. There also appears to have been a decline in

Table 6.1 Average annual growth rates in productivity measures in selected countries: 1960–73 and 1973–9 (in percentages)

Country and time period	Output/ labor	Output/ capital	Total factor productivity
United States			
1960–73	3.1	−0.1	1.9
1973–9	1.1	−0.2	0.6
Canada			
1960–73	4.2	1.1	2.9
1973–9	1.0	−1.6	−0.1
Japan			
1960–73	9.9	0.1	6.6
1973–9	3.8	−2.2	1.8
United Kingdom			
1960–73	3.8	−0.7	2.2
1973–9	1.9	−2.6	0.3
France			
1960–73	5.9	0.7	3.9
1973–9	4.2	−1.1	2.1
West Germany			
1960–73	5.8	−1.5	3.2
1973–9	4.3	−1.9	2.1
Italy			
1960–73	7.8	1.3	5.8
1973–9	1.6	−0.8	0.8
Sweden			
1960–73	5.8	0.1	3.6
1973–9	2.5	−3.3	0.3
Belgium			
1960–73	6.1	0.9	4.2
1973–9	4.4	−0.6	2.6

Source: Kendrick (1982).

total factor-productivity growth in the 1960s, compared to the 1950s, in West Germany, Italy, and the United States.

In the Soviet Union, total factor productivity growth declined from 1960 to 1975. The average annual growth rate during the period 1950–60 was 3.36 percent, 1.83 percent during the period 1960–70, and 0.26 percent during the period 1970–5, as reported by Bergson (1983). This declining trend has continued at least through the early 1980s.

Table 6.3 presents total factor productivity growth rates for eighteen OECD countries. Caution must be exercised when comparing the growth rates in Table 6.3 to those in Tables 6.1 and 6.2. The quality of the underlying data collected today by the OECD, compared to the data used in the aforementioned studies, is more accurate and has been adjusted more systematically to account for price and quality changes, as discussed in OECD (2001). Also, what was likely

Table 6.2 Average annual growth rates in total factor productivity: selected countries, time periods, and authors (in percentages)

Country and time period	TFP growth[1]	TFP growth[2]
Canada		
1947–60	1.7	—
1960–73	1.8	—
1964–73	—	3.3
1974–7	—	1.1
France		
1950–60	2.9	—
1960–73	3.0	—
1964–73	—	5.5
1974–7	—	3.6
West Germany		
1950–60	4.7	—
1960–73	3.0	—
1964–73	—	4.2
1974–7	—	3.7
Italy		
1952–60	3.8	—
1960–73	3.1	—
1964–73	—	6.1
1974–7	—	2.0
Japan		
1952–60	3.4	—
1960–73	4.5	—
1964–73	—	9.5
1974–7	—	2.9
Netherlands		
1951–60	2.3	—
1960–73	2.6	—
United Kingdom		
1955–60	1.5	—
1960–73	2.1	—
United States		
1947–60	1.4	—
1960–73	1.3	—
1964–73	—	2.5
1974–7	—	0.7

Sources
1 Christensen et al. (1980).
2 Nadiri and Mohnen (1981).

attributed to residually measured total factor productivity in the 1980s when the then contemporary studies were done is now captured in more accurately measured inputs, thus lowering residually measured total factor productivity growth rates. With that caveat, the data in Table 6.3 clearly indicate that technological change, as approximated by total factor productivity, growth across countries has

Table 6.3 Average annual growth rates in total factor productivity growth: 1990–5 and 1995–9 (in percentages)

Country	1990–5	1995–9
Ireland	4.4	4.6
Finland	3.0	3.6
Belgium	1.3	1.6
Australia	1.4	1.5
Denmark	1.5	1.5
Netherlands	1.9	1.5
Iceland	1.2	1.4
Canada	1.1	1.3
Sweden	1.3	1.3
United States	1.0	1.2
Norway	2.1	1.2
France	0.9	1.1
Germany	1.1	1.1
United Kingdom	0.8	1.0
Japan	1.3	0.9
Italy	1.2	0.8
New Zealand	1.0	0.7
Spain	0.9	0.5

Source: OECD (2000a).

been relatively stable – increasing in some countries and decreasing in others – during the 1990s.

One point that is clear from a comparison of the three tables above, caveats aside, is that the more interesting issue is the productivity slowdown in the late 1970s. Why did the slowdown occur? How have researchers explored answers to this question, and what did they conclude? How have their answers influenced the course of technology policy? Some answers to all of these questions are reviewed in Chapter 7, but to set the stage, since most of the relevant research was specific to the experience in the United States, productivity growth trends in the United States during these earlier periods are first reviewed in more depth.

The US experience

More detailed data on productivity growth rates were available for the United States than for other OECD countries during the time periods in question. Of course, that is no longer the case given the exceptional data collection efforts that currently exist at the OECD and at other organizations.

Consider the data in Table 6.4. Data for three broad sectors of the US economy are listed in the table. The productivity slowdown appears to have begun in the mid-1960s and to have accelerated after 1973. Moreover, it appears to have been

46   Trends in productivity growth

Table 6.4 Average annual growth rates in productivity measures in the US economy: selected years (in percentages)

Sectors	Output / labor			Output / capital			Total factor productivity		
	1948–76	1948–66	1966–76	1948–76	1948–66	1966–76	1948–76	1948–66	1966–76
Private business sector	3.0	3.5	1.9	1.1	1.5	0.3	2.3	2.9	1.4
Manufacturing sector	2.7	2.9	2.2	0.3	1.0	−0.9	2.1	2.5	1.4
Farm sector	5.0	5.3	4.5	−0.2	−0.6	0.6	3.0	3.5	2.2

Source: Kendrick and Grossman (1980).

quite pervasive across sectors. For example, the average annual rate of growth of labor productivity in the private business sector between the periods 1948–66 and 1966–76 fell from 3.5 percent to 1.9 percent, capital productivity fell from 1.5 percent to 0.3 percent, and total factor productivity fell from 2.9 percent to 1.4 percent. This declining trend also appeared in the manufacturing and farm sectors, with the exception that capital productivity increased in the farm sector between the two time periods.

In the private business sector generally, and in the sizable manufacturing sector in particular, the post-1966 slowdown in total factor productivity growth was aggravated after 1973. Norsworthy *et al.* (1979) report that the rate of growth in labor productivity in the private business sector fell from 3.3 percent between 1948 and 1965, to 2.3 percent between 1965 and 1973, to 1.2 percent between 1973 and 1978. Total factor productivity growth between 1973 and 1978 was lower than in any post-Second World War period, or in fact, as documented by Kendrick (1980) in any period except The Great Depression since the turn of the century.

Average annual total factor productivity growth rates were also estimated during these periods at the two-digit US manufacturing level. As seen from Table 6.5, there is a significant amount of inter-industry variation in growth rates, both for any given time interval as well as between time intervals. In general, the declining trend in manufacturing growth rates was led by primary product industries. Of course, one problem with analyzing such short periods of change is that they are not standardized business cycle phases.

Measurement error and the recent acceleration in US productivity

There has been some research that seeks to determine whether the recent acceleration in US manufacturing productivity is a real phenomenon. Siegel and Griliches (1992) investigated whether the sharp increase in measured manufacturing productivity growth in the 1980s was an overstatement of true productivity growth. Several authors, such as Denison (1989) and Mishel (1988), had previously claimed

Table 6.5 Average annual growth rates in total factor productivity in US manufacturing industries (in percentages)

Industry	1948–53	1953–7	1957–60	1960–6	1966–9	1969–73	1973–6
Food	3.3	2.5	1.1	4.0	1.1	2.8	3.7
Tobacco	1.1	3.5	4.8	2.0	3.6	3.0	1.1
Textiles	0.8	3.6	1.9	8.2	0.1	2.7	0.7
Apparel	2.8	1.4	1.9	2.0	0.8	5.5	2.5
Lumber	0.4	5.8	1.5	7.2	1.6	4.9	−4.7
Furniture	2.2	2.7	0.1	2.7	2.0	1.0	0.8
Paper	3.7	−0.4	1.7	2.8	2.7	5.3	−3.5
Printing, publishing	2.2	2.8	0.6	3.1	0.2	0.7	−1.0
Chemicals	1.8	4.3	2.5	5.0	2.9	4.7	−0.9
Petroleum	1.8	0.6	5.4	4.1	0.8	2.3	−1.7
Rubber	2.1	−2.4	5.7	3.6	3.2	1.4	−1.5
Leather	−2.0	0.7	3.0	3.1	−0.3	2.1	1.2
Stone, clay, glass	2.4	0.1	1.1	2.4	0.8	1.7	−0.9
Primary metals	3.2	−1.5	−4.1	3.3	−3.1	1.8	−3.9
Fabricated metals	1.4	0.3	2.0	2.6	1.5	0.9	−0.9
Machinery, ex. electrical	2.5	−1.9	1.1	2.6	−0.2	2.3	−0.5
Electrical machinery	4.4	2.0	2.6	6.2	2.9	3.7	1.6
Transportation equipment	3.2	1.5	3.3	4.2	−0.5	2.7	3.0
Instruments	4.6	0.6	3.0	3.5	3.1	−0.4	0.1
Miscellaneous	4.0	3.3	2.6	1.6	3.1	2.8	1.6

Source: Kendrick and Grossman (1980).

that this improvement in economic performance was a statistical mirage due to systematic underestimation of input growth caused by increases in foreign and domestic outsourcing, changes in the quality of the workforce, and investment in computers. The evidence presented in the Siegel and Griliches article was not consistent with this hypothesis.

Siegel (1995) extended this research approach by constructing a set of proxy variables to test for measurement errors in output, labor, and materials, and then computing a variety of parametric and non-parametric estimates of TFP. His findings implied that the acceleration in manufacturing productivity growth in the 1980s could not be attributed to measurement error. Elsewhere, Siegel (1994), extending a methodology developed by Lichtenberg and Griliches (1989), examined the incidence of measurement errors in output prices caused by incomplete adjustments for quality change. Estimating several variants of latent variables, or multi-indicators multiple causes model, he found that the producer price index, which was used to construct measures of TFP, missed about 40 percent of quality change. However, these errors appear to be constant over time. Thus, all three of

48   Trends in productivity growth

these studies reached the same basic conclusion: it is likely that there are errors in measuring output and input prices. However, it is not clear that these errors are getting worse over time, or that they can explain major shifts in productivity, such as the productivity slowdown in the 1970s or the acceleration in manufacturing productivity in the 1980s. We discuss the issue of errors of measurement in later chapters.

7 The productivity slowdown

The issue in context

Productivity growth is a fundamental contributor to overall economic well-being. Because of this, the persistent slowdown in productivity growth that began in the mid-1960s in many industrialized countries, that increased in the early 1970s, and that lasted into the 1980s, caused considerable concern at that time and upon reflection even today. An understanding of the causes and correlates of the slowdown is important and fundamental to this volume for several reasons. First, it has historical economic significance, and for that alone it should remain in focus for those who study technological change and productivity growth. Second, the research at that time made important discoveries about the linkage between technological change and productivity growth, emphasizing the role of R&D activity. Third, the findings from that literature, which were reviewed completely in the 1987 monograph and selectively here, set the stage for much of the technology policy of OECD countries. Finally, fourth, as important as this productivity slowdown literature is to the evolution of the field, its limitations have brought about a provocative body of thought related to alternative sources of knowledge and their relationship to technological change – and that body of literature is discussed in detail in Chapter 8.

A critical question, and one that puzzled economists and policy makers at that time was: Why did productivity growth decline at that particular point in time? Was there a structural change such that traditionally measured productivity indices are biased? Had the work ethic of the labor force deteriorated during the 1960s? Was it by chance that the productivity slowdown appears to have coincided with the world energy crisis in 1973–4? Had the pool of potential productivity-enhancing innovations dried-up? Is the productivity slowdown part of a longer-run cycle? Or, is the measured slowdown nothing more than a statistical artifact?

The last of these questions is very important, especially given the measurement issues discussed in the previous chapters regarding production inputs and output. Was there really a slowdown? The data presented in Chapter 6, although highly aggregated, clearly indicate that the slowdown did occur and that it was globally pervasive. Writing at that time, Henrici (1981: 123) asked: "Are we dealing with

50 *The productivity slowdown*

a sick patient or a sick stethoscope?" Darby (1984), among others, answered that the stethoscope was sick.

As noted in Chapter 5, a number of microeconomic-based production studies have clearly indicated that the size of the estimated residual, $A(t)$, diminished when input quality adjustments were made. But, Rees (1980) observed, for such data problems to be the sole contributor to the measured slowdown implied that downward-biasing quality mismeasurement must have been growing substantially during the 1970s. The opposite is more likely, however.

As noted earlier, there have been attempts to assess the extent of these measurement errors over time. One potential source of mismeasurement is the so-called new goods bias, which is addressed theoretically in Diewert (1987) and empirically in Berndt *et al.* (1993). Evidence presented in Siegel (1994), which makes use of detailed product-level data on prices, suggests that while the new goods bias is severe at any point in time, it does not appear as though the mismeasurement of prices is getting worse over time.

As a general rule, the post-productivity slowdown literature attempted to explain the post-1965 or post-1973 productivity slowdown. This was accomplished mainly by correcting partial or total factor productivity growth estimates for changes in efficiency-related factors that are embodied in inputs, but were instead relegated statistically to the residual. These authors also attempted to control for exogenous shocks in the economy that presumably altered the form of the underlying production function. The fact that so many corrections to the conventional productivity statistics have been attempted by so many researchers underscored then and underscores now the importance of fully understanding the simplifying assumptions behind a productivity index before interpreting the index for what it is or what it is not.

Contributing factors: a menu of variables

Several factors related to the productivity growth slowdown are discussed below. Although most researchers agree that each of these factors was important, there still remains some disagreement as to the degree of importance of each. This disagreement results in part from different econometric models and techniques, and from differences in data measurement. The following discussion focuses heavily on the US productivity slowdown. This emphasis characterizes the scope of the literature at that time.

Cyclical shocks

Nordhaus (1980) suggested that the post-1973 slowdown in the United States, while severe, was not unprecedented. His analysis of output per worker in the nonfarm business economy between 1912 and 1979 led him to the conclusion that such slowdowns should be expected from time to time when one takes a long-run view. This conclusion is not inconsistent with Verdoorn's (1980) Law, which predicts a long-run relationship between growth rates of productivity and output.

Others agreed at that time that there are cyclical patterns in labor productivity estimates, but they did not denigrate the importance of the then recent slowdown. The fundamental issue hinged on whether the causes of the slowdown were cyclical – that is, due to changes in the composition of demand or to the utilization of inputs – or secular in nature – that is due to intersectoral or demographic changes in inputs and technology-related investment behavior.

As with many of the empirical analyses that attempted to explain the productivity slowdown, the results and interpretations of the results are mixed. Gordon (1979) argued that part of the post-1965 slowdown in US labor productivity growth was due to an end-of-expansion phenomenon brought about by cyclical labor hiring practices, that is, there is a lag between the output slowdown and the labor-hiring slowdown. However, Dickens' (1982) empirical analysis of changes in labor productivity from 1954 to 1980 suggested that Gordon's end of expansion hypothesis be rejected in favor of the hypothesis that there was a permanent productivity loss during the business cycle downturns that was not regained during the upturn of the corresponding cycles that began in 1966, 1973, and again in 1977. Allen and Link (1984) argued that, as Gordon's analysis would imply, the cyclical component of the productivity slowdown dominated whatever secular trend might have existed during those upturns. Allen and Link found no permanent productivity loss. More generally, Nadiri and Mohnen (1981) had found that about one-half of the measured slowdown in total factor productivity between the two time periods 1964–73 and 1974–7 in the United States, Japan, Canada, France, Germany, and Italy was related to the then prevailing economic recession.

Most of the remaining empirical research in this area has been based on the implicit assumption that the US productivity slowdown – labor productivity growth slowdown and total factor productivity growth slowdown – was due to secular changes brought about either by shocks to the economy or imposed by regulations. A number of such secular changes are discussed below.

Capital investments

Cyclical activity in an economy indirectly affects productivity growth by affecting capital investment. Changes in the growth of capital are frequently cited as an independent causal factor explaining the productivity slowdown.

The framework for these analyses varies. For example, Maddison (1984) compared the average annual rate of growth of domestic production per man-hour to that of capital per employee in six countries between the two time periods 1960–73 and 1973–80. Based on the data in Table 7.1, he concluded that a slowdown in capital formation was one factor that explained the productivity slowdown. In contrast, Kendrick (1982) reached a similar conclusion for nine OECD countries between similar periods of time, 1960–73 and 1973–9.

With respect to the US economy, the size of capital's role in explaining the labor productivity growth slowdown changed after 1973. Prior to 1973, there was general agreement that the slowdown was due less to a weakness in capital formation than to a decline in total factor productivity growth. For example, the growth rate

The productivity slowdown

Table 7.1 Average annual growth rates in productivity-related variables: selected countries, 1960–73 and 1973–81 (in percentages)

Country	GDP per man-hour	Capital stock per employee	Adjusted capital stock per employee
France			
1960–73	5.5	4.8	—
1973–81	3.0	4.5	3.9
West Germany			
1960–73	5.4	6.2	—
1973–81	3.7	4.7	4.1
Japan			
1960–73	9.3	10.6	—
1973–81	3.1	5.8	5.2
Netherlands			
1960–73	5.4	5.9	—
1973–81	2.6	3.4	2.9
United Kingdom			
1960–73	3.9	4.2	—
1973–81	2.9	3.4	2.8
United States			
1960–73	2.6	2.1	—
1973–81	1.1	1.0	0.4

Source: Maddison (1984).

of labor productivity decreased by 1.0 percentage point in the private business sector between the time periods 1948–65 and 1965–73, declining from an annual rate of growth of 3.3–2.3 percent. Norsworthy *et al.* (1979) calculated that 95 percent of the decline between these two time periods was due to changes in factors other than capital and labor. Fraumeni and Jorgenson (1980, 1981) reached a similar conclusion by comparing the 1948–68 and 1968–76 time periods.

The growth-accounting frameworks used in these studies are based on an extension of the generalized production function from equation (4.39):

$$Q = F(K, L, t) \tag{7.1}$$

and from the generalized definition of the index of residually measured technological change from equation (4.40):

$$\frac{A'}{A} = \frac{\partial Q/\partial t}{Q} - v_K \left\{ \frac{\partial K/\partial t}{K} \right\} - v_L \left\{ \frac{\partial L/\partial t}{L} \right\} = v_t, \tag{7.2}$$

where previously we have denoted the distributive share of capital as $\alpha = v_K$ and the distributive share of labor as $\beta = v_L$ – notations change over time and across authors. It follows mathematically from equation (7.2), by subtracting the rate of growth of labor from both sides of the equations and rearranging terms, that:

$$\left\{\frac{\partial Q/\partial t}{Q} - \frac{\partial Q/\partial t}{L}\right\} = v_K\left\{\frac{\partial K/\partial t}{K} - \frac{\partial L/\partial t}{L}\right\} + v_t. \quad (7.3)$$

The left-hand side of equation (7.3) is the rate of growth in labor productivity, that is, the percentage rate of change in Q/L. The first term on the right-hand side is the rate of growth in the capital-to-labor ratio, weighted by the distributive share of capital, v_K, and v_t is total factor productivity growth. The decline in labor productivity growth between the two time periods 1948–65 and 1965–73, or between 1948–68 and 1968–76 depending on the study, was due primarily to a decline in total factor productivity growth, v_t. In fact, Baily (1981a) provided some of the earliest empirical evidence that the rate of growth in the capital-to-labor ratio increased between the two time periods, especially in the manufacturing sector.

There is empirical evidence that the continued slowdown in labor productivity growth after 1973 was due in large part to a decline in capital formation. According to Norsworthy *et al.* (1979), the decline in capital formation accounted for about 70 percent of the decline in labor productivity in the private business sector between the two time periods 1965–73 and 1973–8.

There are several important issues regarding the measurement of the capital stock that are fundamental to the formation of productivity indices. Capital is heterogeneous; it includes equipment, structures, land, and inventories. One measurement issue is related to the method by which these components, and others, are aggregated. Direct aggregation consists of adding the various asset components in constant dollars. Alternatively, a translog or Divisia index is based on adding the growth rates of the assets, weighted by their distributive shares. The difference between the growth rate in the translog index, $\{(\partial K^T/\partial t)/K^T\}$, and the directly aggregated index, $\{(\partial K/\partial t)/K\}$, is the growth rate of factors influencing the effective input of capital services, q_K, as:

$$q_K = \frac{\partial K^T/\partial t}{K^T} - \frac{\partial K/\partial t}{K}. \quad (7.4)$$

A similar index of the growth rate of factors influencing the effective input of labor services is:

$$q_L = \frac{\partial L^T/\partial t}{L^T} - \frac{\partial L/\partial t}{L}. \quad (7.5)$$

Accounting for quality changes that result in effective capital and effective labor differing from measured capital and measured labor leads to a revised version of equation (7.3) as:

$$\frac{\partial Q/\partial t}{Q} - \frac{\partial L/\partial t}{L} = v_K\left\{\frac{\partial K/\partial t}{K} - \frac{\partial L/\partial t}{L}\right\} + v_K q_K + v_L q_L + v_t. \quad (7.6)$$

54 *The productivity slowdown*

In terms of the growth-accounting studies noted above, and in particular in terms of the Norsworthy *et al.* (1979) study, quality changes in capital include changes in the composition of capital – changes in the asset mix among equipment, structures, land, and inventories; intersectoral shifts in capital; and growth in pollution abatement capital. They estimated that these factors, along with the slowdown in growth of the capital-to-labor ratio, accounted for a significant part of the slowdown in labor productivity growth after 1973.

Baily (1981*a,b*) also showed that capital is an important factor explaining the decline in labor productivity growth since 1973. He argued that the flow of capital services relative to the capital stock changed after that date. Although the absolute size of the capital stock was relatively large during the 1970s, its economic value deteriorated due to obsolescence, perhaps resulting from the energy crisis that rendered some capital economically inefficient. Along these same lines, Maddison (1984) adjusted cross-country capital estimates to incorporate the so-called Baily effect. Maddison found, as shown in Table 7.1, that labor productivity growth, measured as gross domestic production per manhour, declined after 1973 in each of the six countries considered, and that growth in the capital-to-labor ratio, adjusted by changes in the economic value of capital, grew slower after 1973 than the unadjusted ratio. This issue is revisited below.

A related measurement issue concerns depreciation of the capital stock. There is a precedent in the literature for using both the gross stock of capital and the net of depreciation stock of capital when measuring real capital inputs. Analyses of data prior to 1973 are not sensitive to the choice of measurement; however, after 1973 the composition of capital changed away from structure to equipment. The latter asset has a much faster rate of depreciation, which suggests, if capital is not a one-hoss-shay, the net capital stock measures are more appropriate.

Inflation and energy prices

Clark (1981, 1982) documented a strong negative correlation between the inflation rate and labor productivity rate in the US economy as far back as the early 1940s. While this relationship may be spurious, at least according to some, there are sound theoretical reasons for expecting inflationary tendencies to have a dampening impact on productivity growth, as discussed in Clark (1981).

First, during periods of unanticipated and prolonged inflation there is less certainty about the meaning and interpretation of price signals than during a period of stable prices. Because managerial decisions are made in an uncertain climate, there may be efficiency losses as planning horizons shorten. Moreover, forecasting and decision-making in the shortened time frame may be misguided. For example, as input prices rise during inflationary periods, it becomes increasingly difficult to determine what portion of the increase is general and inflation-induced, as opposed to reflecting changes in relative factor costs.

Second, managerial talent may be diverted toward short-run decision-making as a result of increased factor price uncertainty. The ramifications of this may show up in an inability to estimate hurdle rates for investment correctly and also in an altered attitude on the part of managers toward risk taking.

Third, in addition to affecting the choice of an optimal input mix, inflationary tendencies can directly affect capital investments. Depreciation of plant and equipment is based on historical costs. As a result, prolonged periods of inflation will lead to a widened gap between historical costs and economic or effective replacement costs. Thus, current profits and taxes on profits are too high vis-à-vis the level requisite for financing required investments.

One obvious phenomenon linked to the worldwide inflation in the 1970s was the 1973 energy crisis. Some writers contended that the 1973 crisis was the primary influence bringing about the post-1973 productivity slowdown. Siegel (1979: 60), for one, wrote that: "Energy prices stand as the single most important contributor to the 1973 [productivity] break."

It was suggested that the energy shock represented a structural change in production relationships. Rasche and Tatom (1977*a*,*b*), for example, argued that energy is a substitute in production for capital and labor. Partial and total factor productivity growth thus declined in response to the energy price increases that began in 1973. Alternatively, Hudson and Jorgenson (1978*a*,*b*), Norsworthy *et al.* (1979), and Jorgenson (1984) argued that capital and energy are complements in production. Increases in energy prices reduce the demand for capital and thus, decrease investment. Total factor productivity growth consequently falls. Using alternative empirical methods, Siegel (1979), Coen and Hickman (1980), and Filer (1980) found that increased energy prices significantly reduced measured productivity growth.

Comparing productivity growth rates among OECD countries between the two time periods 1960–73 and 1973–9, Lindbeck (1983) found that dramatic macroeconomic disturbances between 1972 and 1974 were important for explaining the post-1973 slowdown. He argued that one key disturbance was the OPEC oil crisis and the input reallocation adjustments that followed.

A number of researchers questioned the energy-shock hypothesis, based on their own empirical analyses. Berndt (1980, 1984), for example, contended that input substitution in response to higher energy prices is a long-run phenomenon, and could not have accounted for the contemporaneous decline in measured productivity growth. Others pointed out that there are very few actual examples of such substitution, and investments continued in energy-intensive sectors. What probably happened, and this is conjectured with the benefit of hindsight, was that the energy shock greatly reduced the economic value of the capital stock. If true, then the rate of growth of conventionally measured capital stock overstated the rate of growth of the effective capital stock, meaning that total factor productivity growth measurements after 1973 were probably biased downward. Baily's (1981*a*,*b*) analysis of the role of capital formation in productivity growth is based on estimates of the effective capital stock, measured by adjusting capital by Tobin's q, a proxy for the market valuation of assets. Therein, Baily concluded that the decline in effective capital formation after 1973 was a major cause of the post-1973 labor productivity growth slowdown.

Government regulation

It was also suggested by Abramovitz (1981) and others at that time that government regulations, environmental and work safety program regulations in particular, reduced measured productivity growth because the compliance costs in the industries affected were absorbed by diverting real financial, technical, and human resources from activities that would otherwise increase output. The adjective "measured" is critical when speaking about the impact of regulation on productivity growth. It is important to note that there are benefits from regulations, such as improvements in the value and quality of life, that are not likely to be captured in the conventionally measured indices. For example, if demand increases in industries providing the capital goods and services used by the regulated industries to meet regulated standards, then measured productivity in the supply industry may increase if economies of scale are realized more fully. If this occurs, the induced productivity gains will be realized in the supplier's $A(t)$ index, rather than being traced as a direct consequence of regulation.

If firms in the affected industries comply with regulation by diverting funds from investments in newer vintages of plant and equipment, then the effective capital-to-labor ratio will fall, as will measured productivity growth. Also, if compliance brings about a reallocation of financial resources from, say, R&D expenditures, then productivity growth will fall. The linkage between R&D and productivity growth is documented in Chapter 9. An alternative to the resources-diversion hypothesis is that regulation simply renders certain production methods no longer economical. No resource allocation would then follow, but the capital-in-use to labor ratio would fall. On the other hand, regulation may induce investment in new, more productive techniques. When in use, these new techniques could increase productivity growth.

Several studies investigated these propositions. At the aggregate level, Christiansen and Haveman (1981) found that between 12 percent and 21 percent of the slowdown in labor productivity in US manufacturing between the two time periods 1958–65 and 1973–7 was due to government regulation *per se*. Other industry-specific studies also found that regulation – environmental, health, and safety regulation in particular – resulted in lower labor productivity growth and total factor productivity growth in the United States during the 1970s, compared with earlier periods. Denison (1979, 1984) and Kendrick (1980, 1982) estimated that environmental regulations in the United States, on aggregate, contributed to about 10 percent of the productivity growth slowdown. Using the relative portion of gross domestic product spent on environmental regulation as an adjustment factor, Kendrick (1982) estimated a greater regulator impact in Japan than in the United States, and the same of a smaller impact in other OECD countries than in the United States.

Another test of the diversion of resources hypothesis was by Link (1982*c*). He estimated that the amount of R&D expenditures directed toward environmental compliance activities by firms in the US chemicals, machinery, and petroleum industries was negatively correlated with residually measured total factor productivity growth.

Unionization

One view of unionism predicts that unions will decrease labor productivity by reducing management's flexibility, introducing inefficient work rules, and limiting compensation based on individual production. In contrast to this view, Freeman and Medoff (1979, 1982, 1984), and other economists have emphasized a collective voice/institutional response view. This group argues that unionism, a form of collective organization, may increase the level of labor productivity. Unions are hypothesized to act as agents for workers by providing a collective voice. Productivity is enhanced through decreased worker turnover and the establishment of grievance procedures, work rules, seniority systems, and the like. In addition, unionization shocks management to reduce inefficiency.

The influence of unions in the post-1965 slowdown is rather opaque. A number of studies have found that total factor productivity growth is negatively related to the level of unionism and to changes in the level of unionism. Relevant to the former finding was, for example, the work of Kendrick and Grossman (1980) and Link (1981, 1982a); relevant to the latter finding was, for example, the work of Hirsch and Link (1984). Along these lines, Link and Siegel (2002) report that workers in unionized coal mines often oppose the adoption of new technologies. More specifically, the authors found that many unionized workers did not want their plants to implement real time control systems, even when they were made aware of the fact that the use of this technology reduces the incidence of injuries and fatalities.

It is possible that a portion of the post-1965 slowdown was due to the negative effects of past union power. Union coverage in the private sector has been declining since the mid-1950s, and, according to Hirsch and Addison (1986), it is doubtful that unionism will play an important limiting role in future productivity growth although such a conclusion is contrary to the Link and Siegel (2002) finding.

Entrepreneurship

Although there have been many conceptualizations of who the entrepreneur is and what he does, one important characteristic of entrepreneurship is an ability to create or deal with disequilibria. In an environment as dynamic as an economy is, constraints are constantly changing. According to Schultz (1980: 443):

> [D]isequilibria are inevitable in [a] dynamic economy. These disequilibria cannot be eliminated by law, by public policy, and surely not by rhetoric. A modern dynamic economy would fall apart if not for the entrepreneurial actions of a wide array of human agents who reallocate their resources and thereby bring their part of the economy back into equilibrium.

This constant readjustment toward equilibrium stimulates productivity growth. According to Klein (1979), the 1970s slowdown in US productivity growth can be viewed in terms of a decline in businessmen's ability or desire to deal with disequilibria.

58 *The productivity slowdown*

Did the productivity slowdown stem from a lack of perception or ability by leaders to exercise entrepreneurial talents? The empirical evidence remains wanting. Hayes and Abernathy (1980: 70) suggested that the rules of the game might have changed in the United States. What could be referred to as managerial myopia may simply be a rational response to either short-run profit incentives or to a market of managers that is in flux:

> [W]e believe that during the past two decades, American managers have increasingly relied on principles which prize analytical detachment and methodological elegance over insight, based on experience, into the subtleties and complexities of strategic decisions. As a result, short-run financial returns have become the overriding criteria for many companies.

The importance of a changing entrepreneurial attitude then, and in any period in the future, may always be in question.

Decline in the rate of return of R&D

In the early 1980s there was great concern among economists and policymakers in the United States regarding the pervasive slowdown in productivity growth and the concomitant decline in the global competitiveness of American firms in key high-technology industries. One of the alleged culprits of this productivity slowdown was a decline in the rate of technological innovation, which is a reflection of declining entrepreneurship. The following excerpt from a US House of Representatives hearing on November 18, 1983 aptly reflects the mindset of policy makers at that time:

> A number of indicators strongly suggest that the position of world technology leadership once firmly held by the United States is declining. The United States, only a decade ago, with only five percent of the world's population, was generating about 75 percent of the world's technology. Now, the U.S. share has declined to about 50 percent and in another ten years, without fundamental changes in our Nation's technological policy ... the past trend would suggest that it may be down to only 30 percent. [In Committee hearings] many distinguished scientific and industry panels had recommended the need for some relaxation of current antitrust laws to encourage the [entrepreneurial] formation of R&D joint ventures. ... The encouragement and fostering of joint research and development ventures are needed responses to the problem of declining U.S. productivity and international competitiveness.

As evident in this quotation, the early 1980s was a period of intense soul-searching in the United States, which ultimately led to some major changes in what became known as the US National Innovation System (Nelson 1993). These changes implied direct financial support to private firms from government agencies for R&D projects, such as the US Commerce Department's Advanced

Technology Program; relaxation of antitrust statutes to promote collaborative R&D, such as the National Cooperative Research Act (NCRA) of 1984; and policies to promote the more rapid diffusion of technology from universities and federal laboratories to private firms, such as the Bayh–Dole Act of 1980.

It is interesting to note that, according to Lichtenberg and Siegel (1991), the empirical evidence suggests that the strength of the connection between R&D and productivity did not actually diminish during the productivity slowdown, at least at the firm level. Of course, this finding does not rule out the possibility that there was a decline in the social returns to R&D during this time period. To the best of our knowledge, no one has ever attempted to assess variation in overall social returns to R&D over time.

A more focused look

Although conceptual and measurement problems are inherent in total factor productivity indices, the post-1965 and post-1973 trends in total factor productivity growth for industrial countries seem sufficiently robust to raise a question whether innovative activity slowed down. A prior question is: What kinds of activities spur innovation?

Although macroeconomic forces, or those forces that shape investment in new technology, have influenced the productivity growth pattern, our story would be limited if we focused exclusively on such factors. For completeness, and also to improve our understanding of current technology policy, we need to focus greater attention on the microfoundations of the relationship between technological change and productivity growth and all relevant linkages. Such a conceptual model of endogenous technical progress is provided in the following chapter.

8 Sources of technical knowledge

An early conceptual model

Figure 8.1 outlines schematically the technology strategies and environmental constraints associated with the sources of a firm's technical knowledge, as prevailed in much of the relevant literature in the late 1970s and throughout the 1980s. Hence, this conceptual model is a useful starting point, although we will criticize this model, and thus the mindset of many of the researchers at the time, later in this chapter. In the model in Figure 8.1, firms are shown to operate in a market environment, which influences their innovative activities. Markets are traditionally characterized in economics on a continuum ranging from monopoly to pure competition. Although this continuum is useful for discussions about price competition or competitive strategy, it loses some applicability when technological competition is considered.

A firm's technological environment can be characterized along several dimensions. The overall market structure in which the firm operates influences its innovation strategy, and that strategy in turn influences the methods used for acquiring, developing, and modifying technology. For example, in mature markets, where

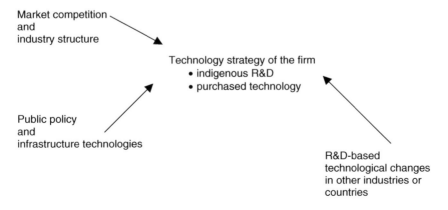

Figure 8.1 Early conceptual model of sources of technical knowledge.

product competition is primarily in terms of price, a firm's technology response may emphasize process-related innovations aimed at reducing operating costs. In an emerging market, product innovation may be the more appropriate strategy.

A relevant strategy decision associated with an innovation stimulus is where to invest in new technology. The firm has two broad, but not necessarily mutually exclusive, choices: it can internalize the innovation process by pursuing specific activities, generally characterized under the rubric of R&D, or it can use existing markets to purchase the requisite technology. The notion of internalizing a market activity for which there exist alternative market mechanisms was first addressed by Coase (1937) in terms of transactions costs. To illustrate his argument, a firm will conduct R&D in-house when the transactions costs are lower than purchasing equivalent technology in the market place. However, that simplistic approach does not hold well with R&D since R&D represents an investment in knowledge and the firm will receive benefits from being able to appropriate that knowledge. Hence, appropriability issues and transactions costs are both relevant in the so-called make-or-buy decision when technology is involved. Timing is also an important factor since the firm may not have sufficient time to develop its own technology if it is to remain competitive in an industry where technology lifecycles are short.

In terms of Figure 8.1, the firm's technology strategy is simply dichotomized between internal or indigenous R&D and purchased technology. As the vintage production-function models surveyed in Chapter 4 and represented in equations (4.37) and (4.38) in particular suggest, the firm can acquire new technology by purchasing new vintages of capital equipment. Hence, this buy strategy is implied within a neo-classical production framework. Bozeman and Link (1983), as shown in Table 8.1, reported data on the relative importance of alternative technology sources. Clearly make is greater than buy, meaning that manufacturing firms in the United States reported in their study that indigenous R&D activity was a relatively more important source than purchased technology embodied in new capital equipment, but technology also enters the firm through mergers and through licensing activities.

Table 8.1 Relative importance of alternative sources of technical knowledge

Source	Mean ranking (1 = very important to 5 = not important at all)
Indigenous R&D activity	1.3
Purchasing new capital equipment	2.7
Acquisition of firms through mergers	3.1
Licensing from domestic firms	3.7
Licensing from international firms	3.8
R&D conducted under government contract	4.2

Source: Bozeman and Link (1983).

62 Sources of technical knowledge

Table 8.2 Relative importance of technical knowledge frequently used by R&D groups in US manufacturing firms

Source	Mean ranking (4 = always used to 1 = never used)
Own marketing group	3.15
Own manufacturing group	3.12
Technical equipment suppliers	2.68
Customers	2.67
Professional interaction with peers outside the firm	2.59
Informal interaction with peers outside the firm	2.49
Universities	2.25
Consulting firms	2.09
National Technical Information Service	1.93
Other government agencies	1.92
Reverse engineering of competitors' products	1.90
New employees hired from competitors	1.81

Source: Link and Zmud (1987).

Even within an internal R&D unit, numerous sources of knowledge are relied upon to enhance the innovation process that occurs within. Link and Zmud (1987) identified twelve sources of technical knowledge used by R&D groups in US manufacturing firms. Table 8.2 lists these sources, along with their reported frequency of use. The most important sources were the firm's own marketing and manufacturing groups. Of course, the firm's choice of which source to rely on for R&D intelligence is guided in large part by the nature of the firm's R&D spending, discussed below. Firms undertaking basic research and reporting an overall imitative, as opposed to an innovative R&D strategy, tend to use external sources more frequently. Internal marketing sources are more frequently used by firms characterized by R&D that is primarily short term in its focus.

An integrated model of the entrepreneurial process

We posit that the schematic in Figure 8.2 captures contemporary thinking about alternative sources of technical knowledge. It is more encompassing than the decades-old model in Figure 8.1 for two reasons. First, it reflects alternative sources of knowledge – and as discussed in Chapter 2 knowledge is the catalyst for technological change – that were little understood in the 1980s, or if understood little emphasized. Second, over time public policies have had time to respond to the productivity slowdown and those responses have become institutionalized and researchers have begun to focus on them.

Figure 8.2 characterizes the firm as the entrepreneurial agent of change, or as stated in the previous chapter, the agent adjusting to disequilibria. The firm, as

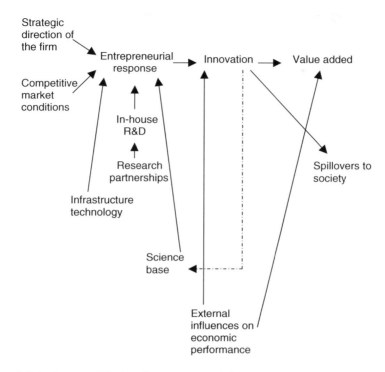

Figure 8.2 An integrated look at the entrepreneurial process.

illustrated by the upper horizontal elements in the figure, optimizes given its strategic focus and the competitive pressures it faces in the market place, and of course the two are interrelated although they are shown separately in the figure. Optimization generates an entrepreneurial response, and that purposive action in turn results in an innovation. There are additional market forces at work that are, in part, beyond the influence of the firm. These forces determine the economic value of the innovation and hence, the value added to the firm as well as to the user of the innovation.

R&D activity is the primary resource that the firm relies upon to investigate the appropriate response and to act upon it. Enhancing the firm's R&D activity is the firm's relationship with other organizations as well as with its external environment. One such relationship is its involvement with other firms, or perhaps with either a university or a federal laboratory, a point to be discussed in Chapter 11. Such strategic associations are frequently referred to as research partnerships. Also, firms rely on infrastructure technology that comes from federal laboratories, or perhaps even from the environment created by being located in a science park. The science base, which consists of the stock of knowledge generated from basic research, resides in the public domain – and the public domain is international

64 *Sources of technical knowledge*

in scope – generally in the form of scientific journals but also it is in part embodied in university scientists.

As illustrated, the result of the entrepreneurial process is innovation. As stated above, an innovation will generate value added if it is accepted in the marketplace. Furthermore, it will diffuse into society and generate spillover benefits to other firms both within the industry and in other industries that ultimately use the innovation. The dashed arrow coming back to the science base shows an internal feedback. Once an innovation exists, knowledge has been created and it too will reside in the public domain.

The usefulness of this illustration is not only as a summary device of alternative sources of technical knowledge that affect the firm's innovative behavior, which in turn is associated with technological change and then productivity growth, which in turn affects economic performance, but also it is an effective template for summarizing technology policies.

Dimensions of R&D

There are three fundamental dimensions of R&D, and R&D is the driving investment in the model in Figure 8.2. The first dimension concerns the source of funding of R&D, that is to who finances the investment. A second aspect relates to the performance of R&D, that is to who conducts the research and development. The third dimension concerns the character of use of R&D, that is whether the investment activity is of a basic or applied nature, or development. These three fundamental dimensions are not mutually exclusive. In addition to these dimensions, there are also two other important aspects of R&D. One aspect is the relationship between the size of firms and its propensity to conduct R&D, and the second aspect is the relationship between R&D and total factor productivity growth, which is the topic of Chapter 9.

Sources of funding of R&D

In most industrialized countries, industry accounts for the majority source of funding for R&D. In Japan, industry's percentage is the greatest, followed by Germany and the United States, all over 60 percent. Exceptions are Italy and Russia where the government is the greatest source of R&D funding.

In the United States, industry currently funds about 70 percent of R&D, but the primacy of industry in funding R&D has not always held. In the aftermath of the Second World War until the early 1980s, the federal government was the leading provider of R&D funds in the nation. Although a federal R&D presence was in existence before then, during the Second World War the federal government dramatically expanded its R&D effort by establishing a network of federal laboratories, specifically including atomic weapons laboratories. It was at that time that the federal government also greatly increased its support to extramural R&D performers, especially to a select group of universities and large industrial firms.

After the Second World War, federal R&D support continued to expand for both defense and non-defense purposes, including health R&D in the National Institutes of Health and – after the establishment of the National Science Foundation in 1950 – a broad portfolio of fundamental research activities. As a result of a post-Sputnik national commitment to catch up to the Soviet space successes, federal support for space-related R&D mushroomed in the late 1950s and early 1960s. By 1960 the federal government accounted for 65 percent of the nation's total investment – 80 percent of which was for defense – and industry accounted for 32 percent of the total. Over the next twenty years the federal government continued to be the leading source of R&D funding, although the direction of its funding shifted away from defense over time. By 1970, however, after the success of several lunar landings, support for other non-defense purposes began to claim an increasingly larger share of the federal R&D totals, and continued to do so throughout the 1970s; notably growth in federal energy R&D occurred as a response to the several oil embargoes. Also by 1970, R&D support from industry was on the rise – in part in response to the productivity slowdown – and it accounted for just over 40 percent of the total national R&D effort. As a result of relatively flat federal funding in the 1970s and continual slow growth from the industrial sector, the federal government and industry accounted for about equal shares by the early 1980s.

R&D performers

In the United States, and in most industrialized countries, R&D is performed in what has been called the US national innovation system (Nelson 1993). The system's many dimensions have been widely studied; according to Crow and Bozeman (1998: 42), the US national innovation system could be thought of as "the complex network of agents, policies, and institutions supporting the process of technical advance in an economy."

The venue for the performance of R&D within the system – and this is also true in all industrial nations – are research laboratories. The laboratory performers of R&D correspond to the sectors that finance R&D, but not all R&D funded by a sector is performed in that sector.

Almost one-third of US R&D funded by the federal government is performed in industry, and more than one-half of these funds are spent in the aircraft, missiles, and transportation equipment industries. Universities and colleges fund only about 20 percent of the R&D they perform in their laboratories. Over one-half of R&D performed in universities and colleges comes from the federal government and the rest equally from industry, non-profit institutions, and non-federal government sources.

Foreign investments in R&D are not unique to US firms; the outflow of US industrial R&D into other countries is approximately offset by an inflow of others' R&D to be performed in the United States. More than one-half of US-funded R&D abroad was performed in Europe – primarily in Germany, the United Kingdom, and France. Overall, US R&D investments abroad have generally shifted away from

66 *Sources of technical knowledge*

the larger European countries and Canada, and toward Japan, several of the smaller European countries such as Sweden and the Netherlands, Australia, and Brazil.

Substantial R&D investments are made by foreign firms in the United States. From 1987 to 1996, inflation-adjusted R&D growth from majority-owned affiliates of foreign firms averaged almost 11 percent per year, and are now roughly equivalent to US companies' R&D investment abroad. Affiliates of firms domiciled in Germany, Switzerland, the United Kingdom, France, and Japan collectively account for nearly three-fourths of this foreign funding. Foreign-funded R&D in the United States is concentrated in drugs and medicines mostly from Swiss, German, and British firms; industrial chemicals funded predominantly by German and Dutch firms; and electrical equipment predominantly from French affiliates.

R&D by character of use

Vannevar Bush (1945) is credited for first using the term "basic research." In his 1945 report to President Roosevelt, *Science – the Endless Frontier*, Bush used that term and defined it to mean research conducted without thought of practical ends. Since then, policy makers world wide have been concerned about definitions that appropriately characterize the various aspects of scientific inquiry that broadly fall under the label of R&D and that relate to the linear model that Bush proffered.

Definitions are important to the OECD as well as, in the United States, to the National Science Foundation (NSF) because it, like counterpart organizations such as Statistics Canada, collects expenditure data on R&D. For those data to reflect accurately industrial and academic investments in technological advancement, and for those data to be comparable over time, there must be a consistent set of reporting definitions.

The classification scheme used by the NSF for reporting purposes was developed for its first industrial survey in 1953–4, as documented in Link's (1996*b*) history of the NSF R&D classification scheme. While minor definitional changes were made in the early years, namely to modify the category originally referred to as basic or fundamental research to simply basic research, the concepts of basic research, applied research, and development have remained much as was implicitly contained in Bush's 1945 so-called linear model:

$$\text{Basic Research} \to \text{Applied Research} \to \text{Development}. \tag{8.1}$$

The objective of basic research is to gain more comprehensive knowledge or understanding of the subject under study, without specific applications in mind. Basic research is defined as research that advances scientific knowledge but does not have specific immediate commercial objectives, although that knowledge may be in fields of present or potential commercial interest. Much of the scientific research that takes place at universities is basic research. Applied research is aimed at gaining the knowledge or understanding to meet a specific recognized need. Applied research includes investigations oriented toward discovering new scientific knowledge that has specific commercial objectives with respect to products, processes, or services. Development is the systematic use of the knowledge or understanding gained from research directed toward the production of useful materials, devices, systems, or methods, including the design and development of prototypes and processes.

Development is the largest category of R&D spending in industrial nations and basic research is the least. While allocation percentages vary by country, in general about one-half or more is development with the majority of the rest going to applied research.

R&D activity in small and large firms

Firm-specific data on R&D expenditures for small-sized companies are not readily available in the United States; however, aggregate National Science Foundation data show that over one-half of the amount that industry currently spends on R&D was performed in firms with 10,000 or more employees; less than one-fiftieth was performed in firms with fewer than 500 employees.

Stylized facts aside, there is a more subtle and perhaps more important R&D-related issue. Since the early 1980s, in response to the productivity growth slowdown, policy makers have been concerned that American firms in key industries were losing their dominance of global markets. During the 1990s, these same industries seem to have reemerged as major international competitors. While some of this resurgence is a response to purposive policies, a portion of it can also be attributable to small firms, many of which were not in existence in the early 1980s to be affected by policy and many of which do not even conduct R&D. Still, during the 1990s, small firms were a driving engine of growth, job creation, and renewed global competitiveness through innovation.

There is a rich literature related to the performance of R&D in small firms as compared to large firms. Some of the conclusions from this research, and these conclusions apply to European countries as well where the relevant distinction is not large sized and small sized, but large-sized and small and medium-sized enterprises (SME), are as follows. Large firms have a greater propensity to patent than small firms. Small firms are just as innovative as large firms, in general. However, in some industries, large firms have the innovative advantage (pharmaceuticals, aircraft), while in other industries small firms have the innovative advantage (software, biotechnology). And, small-firm and large-firm innovative activities are complementary.

Table 8.3 is a selected summary of the findings from the literature on innovation and firm size.

The economic importance of small firms, including the innovative differences between small firms and large firms, requires an explanation since the share of overall economic activity attributable to small firms is small and it did not

68 Sources of technical knowledge

Table 8.3 Selected studies of the relationship between innovation and firm size

Innovation measure	Finding	Author
R&D	R&D spending is positively related to firm size	Mueller (1967) Grabowski (1968) Mansfield (1968)
Research partnership with universities	Positive relationship between firm size and likelihood of being involved with a university as a research partner	Link and Rees (1990)
Patents	Patenting is positively or proportionally related to firm size	Scherer (1965a, 1983a) Pakes and Griliches (1980) Hall et al. (1986) Schwalback and Zimmermann (1991)
New product innovations	Parity across firm size, although there are differences according to industry	Acs and Audretsch (1990) Audretsch (1995)
Adoption of advanced manufacturing technologies	Positive relationship between firm size and the probability of adopting an advanced manufacturing technology	Romeo (1975) Dunne (1994) Siegel (1999)

increase during the 1990s. The explanation relevant to the focus of this book begins with a model of the knowledge production function first set forth by Griliches (1979).

As will be discussed in Chapter 9, a production function can meaningfully be expanded conceptually and analytically to include the stock of knowledge as a discrete input along with K and L. One investment in knowledge that many firms make is in R&D. However, there are other key factors that generate knowledge for the firm besides R&D. In fact, many small firms do not formally conduct R&D, yet they are very innovative. Such firms rely on knowledge that spills over from external sources including universities, and small firms are relatively more adept at absorbing knowledge from external sources than large firms. Table 8.4 provides a brief summary of this spillover literature with respect to small firms.

Included in Table 8.4 under the source category of individual spillovers – and economists and policy makers use the term "spillover" to refer to the diffusion of an economic good or economic activity, either intentionally or unintentionally due to market failure – are new employees. An interesting question is: Why are small firms able to exploit knowledge embodied in new employees to a greater extent than large firms? One answer is that new and small firms provide the opportunity for creative individuals to implement new ideas that otherwise would be rejected or would remain unexploited in an organizationally rigid firm. New firms thus serve as agents of change. In a global economy where comparative advantage is based in large part on innovation, small firms are a critical resource.

Table 8.4 Selected studies of knowledge spillovers

Spillover source	Finding	Author
Industry spillovers	Spillovers vary across industries; greater spillovers in knowledge-intensive industries	Jaffe (1989) Saxenian (1990) Acs et al. (1992) Jaffe et al. (1993) Audretsch and Feldman (1996) Morrison and Siegel (1997)
University spillovers	University knowledge spillovers more important to small firms than large firms	Link and Rees (1990) Audretsch and Feldman (1996)
	Knowledge spillovers from university research partners create research awareness and help firms assimilate basic research results	Hall et al. (2000, forthcoming)
Firm spillovers	Firm spillovers more important to large firms than small firms	Acs et al. (1994) Feldman (1994) Eden et al. (1997)
	Knowledge spillovers through licensing greater in more diversified firms	Link and Scott (2000a)
	Publicly funded additions to the stock of knowledge stimulates firm R&D	Jaffe (1989) Adams (1990)
Federal laboratory spillovers	CRADAs are the primary channel through which federal laboratories increase patenting and R&D of firms	Adams et al. (2000)
City spillovers	Industrial diversity generates more spillovers than specialization; localized competition more than monopoly	Glaeser et al. (1992) Almeida and Kogut (1997)
Individual spillovers	Spillovers shaped by role and mobility of knowledge workers	Audretsch and Stephan (1996) Prevezer (1997)

9 The technology–productivity growth relationship

A framework for analysis

Since the early 1960s, researchers have conducted empirical analyses of the impact of investment in R&D on productivity and productivity growth. The framework used by most researchers begins with a Solow-like (1957) model. A generalized version of this early model is, following Griliches (1979), discussed in this chapter.

A generalizable production function applicable to the ith firm, ith industry, ith sector, or the economy, can be written as:

$$Q_i = A_i \, F(K, L, T)_i, \tag{9.1}$$

where, as in all of the production functions discussed in this volume, Q represents output. This model is commonly referred to in the literature (see Griliches and Lichtenberg (1984)) as the R&D capital stock model. In equation (9.1), A is a neutral disembodied shift factor. That is, it is not written here specifically as a function of time, t, as in previous chapters because many applications of equation (9.1) are to cross-sectional data. The stock of physical capital and labor or human capital are K and L, respectively. The stock of technical capital available to the unit of observation, hereafter referred to as the firm for simplicity, is represented as T. T in turn can be written in terms of the alternative sources upon which the firm, acquires technical knowledge, as illustrated in Figure 8.2.

Although this extended model in equation (9.2) has most often been applied in an abbreviated form primarily because of data limitations, its general representation includes four sources of technical knowledge, each corresponding conceptually to sources illustrated in Figure 8.2. Following Charles River Associates (1981) and Tassey (1982):

$$T_i = G(OT_i, PT_i, GT_i, IT), \tag{9.2}$$

where OT_i is the ith firm's own or self-financed stock of technical knowledge, PT_i is the ith firm's purchased stock of technical knowledge, GT_i is the ith firm's government-financed stock of technical knowledge, and IT is the infrastructure technology that the ith firm utilizes in its production of technology process. Note that there is no firm subscript on IT since it, as discussed below, is public domain technology.

As is most common in the literature, OT_i is assumed to be the relevant source of technical knowledge affecting the firm's productivity, and further it is assumed to be related to the ith firm's internal or self-financed previous R&D expenditures, RD, as:

$$OT_i = \sum a_{i,j} RD_{i,t-j}, \tag{9.3}$$

where the ith firm's accumulation weights, a_j, reflect the influence of a j-period distributed lag and obsolescence rate of R&D.

Early empirical studies of the technology-productivity growth relationship were based on a simplified version of the model in equation (9.3) where the only argument defining T_i was OT_i and the production function was Cobb–Douglas:

$$Q = A\, e^{\lambda t}\, K^\alpha\, L^{(1-\alpha)}\, T^\beta, \tag{9.4}$$

where λ is a disembodied rate of growth parameter and α and β are output elasticities. Constant returns to scale are assumed with respect to K and L, but not with respect to T.

Using logarithmic transformations, as in Chapter 4, and differentiating the resulting version of equation (9.4) with respect to time, t, one obtains:

$$\frac{Q'}{Q} = \frac{\partial Q/\partial t}{Q} = \lambda + \alpha \frac{\partial K/\partial t}{K} + (1-\alpha)\frac{\partial L/\partial t}{L} + \beta \frac{\partial T/\partial t}{T}. \tag{9.5}$$

Residually measured productivity growth is defined, as originally done in equations (4.23) and (4.24) absent T, as:

$$\frac{A'}{A} = \frac{Q'}{Q} - \alpha\frac{\partial K/\partial t}{K} - (1-\alpha)\frac{\partial L/\partial t}{L} = \lambda + \beta\frac{\partial T/\partial t}{T}, \tag{9.6}$$

where as before $A'/A = \{(\partial A/\partial t)/A\}$.

In equations (9.4) and (9.6), the parameter β is the output elasticity of technical capital:

$$\beta = (\partial Q/\partial T)\,(T/Q). \tag{9.7}$$

For $\beta > 0$, equation (9.4) exhibits constant returns to scale in K and L and increasing returns to scale in K, L, and T. Substituting the right-hand side of equation (9.7) into equation (9.6), and rearranging terms, yields:

$$A'/A = \lambda + \rho\,(T'/Q) \tag{9.8}$$

for $T' = (\partial T/\partial t)$ and for $\rho = (\partial Q/\partial T)$. From equation (9.8), ρ is the marginal product of technical capital and T' is the decision-making unit's net private investment in the stock of technical capital.

It was generally assumed in the early empirical work, that the stock of R&D-based technical capital does not depreciate, or if it does depreciate it does so very slowly. Thus T' is reasonably approximated by the flow of self-financed R&D expenditures in a given period of time, RD, as:

$$A'/A = \lambda + \rho\,(RD/Q). \tag{9.9}$$

Empirical estimates of ρ from equation (9.9) have been interpreted as an estimate of the marginal private rate of return to investments in R&D. To the extent that the R&D stock of technical capital does in fact depreciate, such an estimate of the marginal private rate of return is downwardly biased, as demonstrated by Scherer (1982). Also, Schankerman (1981) discusses the impact of double-counting in the calculation of the private returns to R&D, since R&D expenditures are often already included in measures of K and L. Thus, it is common in the later variants of this literature to refer to ρ as an excess rate of return, meaning a rate of return in excess of normal remuneration to conventional factors of production.

The empirical evidence

The large body of literature on estimating equations similar to equation (9.9) can be summarized in various ways. Here, we review relevant studies in a chronological order, based on sample period used by the authors in an effort to better document the evolution of this body of research. Studies focusing on the early post-war decades reported a strong positive relationship between R&D and productivity growth. However, findings reported for later years are mixed. For the most part, these studies have been based on US data.

The 1950s and 1960s

Minasian's (1962) investigation focused on 85 industrial firms over the period 1947 to 1957. Using a simplified version of equation (9.9), he found that R&D spending was a statistically significant determinant of productivity growth in chemical firms. Griliches (1973) reached a similar conclusion from an analysis of two-, three-, and four-digit manufacturing industries between 1958 and 1963. In a subsequent article, Griliches (1980b) extended his analysis to examine a sample of firms during the 1965–75 period. His later results were similar to earlier results in that he found that the R&D-to-productivity growth relationship was positive and statistically significant.

Perhaps the most extensive industry-level investigation of this early time period literature was by Terleckyj (1974). He, too, based on his analysis of two- and three-digit industries, found ρ in equation to be positive and statistically significant. More important than simply adding to the body of empirical literature that

R&D expenditures are an important determinant of productivity growth, he was perhaps the first to go beyond the specification in equation (9.9) to a specification that approached the conceptual representation of a production function using T as defined by equation (9.2). Specifically, he attempted to quantify the impact of interindustry spillovers of technical knowledge by adding to equation (9.9) a variable for government-financed R&D and R&D embodied in purchased inputs, intermediate goods and capital goods specifically. Government-financed R&D had no statistical impact on measured productivity growth but embodied R&D did. One might date the literature on diffusion or spillover – see Chapter 5 – as an indicator of economic performance to this Terleckyj study.

The early 1970s

In the US economy, there was a modest decline in total factor productivity growth until about 1973, which then became more severe and lasted until the end of the decade. This post-1973 decline was especially steep for the manufacturing sector. Meanwhile, industrial R&D spending had begun to decline in both relative and absolute terms during the late 1960s. Not surprisingly, given the empirical research reviewed just above, researchers as well as policy makers focused on the declining R&D spending pattern to identify a technology-based culprit for the 1970s productivity growth slump.

Total US R&D as a percentage of GNP peaked at 3 percent by 1964 and then fell to 2.3 percent by 1975. There was disagreement regarding the quantitative impact of the R&D decline on measured productivity growth. Nadiri (1980) and Nadiri and Schankerman (1981) estimated that the reduced rate of R&D stock accumulation might have accounted for as much as one-third of the post-1973 productivity decline. Denison (1979) and Griliches (1980*a*) averred that the R&D slowdown accounted for at best one-tenth of the decline in productivity growth. Griliches (1980*a*) posited that it was not the slowdown in R&D that was important but rather the collapse in the productivity of R&D itself. But, in subsequent years, based on analyses of newer microeconomic data sets, Griliches' opinion changed. This latter group of studies included the works of Griliches and Mairesse (1984), Cuneo and Mairesse (1984) for French manufacturing firms, and Clark and Griliches (1984). As noted in Chapter 7, Lichtenberg and Siegel (1991) reported that the private, or firm level, returns to company-funded R&D in the United States remained high during the productivity slowdown of the 1970s.

Post-slowdown policy

It is well documented that R&D spending, within the framework that underlies equation (9.9) is positively and statistically significantly correlated with measured productivity growth in the United States and in selected OECD countries. Thus, it is not surprising that policy makers worldwide advocated policies to simulate industrial R&D in an effort to reverse the productivity slowdown that persisted until the early 1980s.

74 The technology–productivity growth relationship

The immediate policy response, and the timing of this response varied by country, was to encourage a higher level of industrial R&D spending. As shown in Table 9.1, R&D and R&D-related tax credits were widely introduced, in many cases because of the overwhelming empirical evidence of the relationship between productivity growth and R&D spending. Simply put, it was believed that a tax credit would lower a firm's marginal cost of conducting R&D and, holding marginal benefits constant, provide firms with an incentive to increase their level of spending. Feldman *et al.* (2002) discuss these credits with reference to the United States. Based on this body of research, including an article by Leyden and Link (1993) and the Hall and van Reenan (2000) synthesis and interpretation of

Table 9.1 Summary of tax policies specific to R&D in various countries

Country	Year enacted	R&D tax credit	Special assistance
Australia	1985	None	150% expensing of R&D and R&D grants
Belgium	?	None	R&D personnel subsidies
Brazil	?	None	R&D profits exempt from taxes
Canada	1960s	20% incremental credit	None
China	?	None	None
Denmark	?	None	None
France	1983	50% incremental credit	R&D investment grants in selected industries
Germany	?	None	R&D investment grants
Ireland	?	None	None
Italy	?	None	None
Korea	?	10 to 25% credit	Expense against future R&D
Japan	1966	20% incremental credit	Trade policies beneficial to R&D equipment
Netherlands	1994	Up to 25% credit	Subsidies for R&D inputs
Norway	?	None	Expense against future R&D
Singapore	?	None	200% expensing of R&D
South Africa	?	None	None
Spain	?	15 to 30% credit	None
Sweden	Until 1984	Was 30% credit	Were subsidies on R&D salaries
Switzerland	?	None	None
Taiwan	?	20% incremental credit	None
United Kingdom	?	None	None
United States	1981	20% incremental credit	None

Note
In many cases there is not sufficient institutional information as to the exact year that the R&D or R&D-related tax credit was enacted, thus a ? appears in the column.

the literature, it is fair to conclude that the literature remains mixed about the effectiveness, across countries, of this policy. This suggests that such tax credits seem to be revenue neutral, that is, that dollar-for-dollar the amount of the credit equals the amount of the increase in R&D spending. The most complete review of this literature is presented in Hall and van Reenen (2000).

Studies that disaggregate R&D

Referring to equation (9.2) and (9.9), the state-of-the-art has, for the most part, been to view privately financed R&D as the primary determinant of productivity growth. This finding appears to be quite robust at the firm and industry levels. This focus on R&D in total was due in large part to the paucity of publicly available data at a microeconomic level on R&D either by character of use – basic research, applied research, and development – or by source of funding – self-financed R&D versus R&D embodied in purchased technology versus government-financed R&D.

As noted above, Terleckyj's (1974) work was pioneering with regard to its attempt to disaggregate R&D using public domain data. Since then a number of studies have extended this avenue of investigation, using primarily survey data. These studies are reviewed in Table 9.2. The most important conclusion to be drawn from these studies is that firms rely on myriad sources of technical knowledge – as conceptualized in Figure 8.2 – and each source does affect not only the firm's productivity growth but also the efficiency with which it conducts R&D. Mansfield (1980) and Link (1981) disaggregated self-financed R&D by character of use and found that the marginal return to basic research was the greatest. Further, Link (1981) disaggregated government-financed R&D by character of use and found that government-financed basic research was statistically more important than government-financed applied research or development at the firm level.

Table 9.2 Disaggregated R&D – productivity growth studies

Author	Level of analysis	Disaggregation of R&D
Terleckyj (1974)	US industries	Government funded R&D
		R&D embodies in purchased capital
Mansfield (1980)	US firms	Private R&D by character of use
Link (1981)	US firms	Private R&D by character of use
		Government R&D by character of use
Link (1982a)	US firms	Product and process R&D
Terleckyj (1982)	US industries	Product and process R&D
Scherer (1982, 1983b)	US industries	Product and process R&D
		R&D embodies in purchased capital
Griliches (1986)	US firms	Private R&D by character of use
		Government R&D by character of use
Lichtenberg and Siegel (1991)	US firms (with productivity estimates based on plant-level data)	Private R&D by character of use
		Government R&D by character of use

Using more recent and more comprehensive data, Lichtenberg and Siegel (1991) also found a productivity premium associated with basic research.

Both the Mansfield and Link studies of self-financed firm R&D by character of use were verified by Griliches' (1986) analysis using an alternative data set.

Link (1982a) and Terleckyj (1982) disaggregated R&D, firm R&D and industry-level R&D respectively, into process-enhancing expenditures and product-development expenditures and found the former had the greater statistical relationship to productivity growth. Their findings were verified by Scherer's (1982, 1983b) industry-level line of business analysis. More importantly, Scherer's work, followed by Link's (1983), emphasized the productivity growth enhancing nature of technology embodied in purchased capital equipment, that is, inter-industry technology flows.

The relationship between government-financed R&D and productivity growth is more complex. The complexity is due to the fact that the impact of government-financed R&D is not independent of its relationship with self-financed R&D. Beginning with Blank and Stigler (1957), scholars have debated the complementarity or pump-priming versus substitution effect between the two. The latter is often referred to as the crowding-out hypothesis. While this literature – extended by Higgins and Link (1981); Link (1982b); Lichtenberg (1984, 1987, 1988); Holemans and Sleuwagen (1988); Antonelli (1989); Leyden et al. (1989); Leyden and Link (1991, 1992); and Wallsten (2000), and reviewed by David et al. (2000) – is important because it emphasizes that alternative technical sources are interrelated and appear to affect productivity growth.

With reference to Figure 8.2, there are three external sources of technical knowledge that have not yet been discussed with reference to the specifications in equations (9.2) and (9.9) that are considered to be important in the technological change and productivity growth literature.

The first source is research partnerships. The US economy did recover from the productivity-growth slowdown, in terms of measured domestic productivity growth in the early to mid-1980s, but so did productivity growth in other countries. Unfortunately for US industry, a nagging consequence of declining industrial R&D and productivity growth was a loss in global market share for many American firms. Although not documented officially until after the fact, the trend in the competitiveness of American industries in emerging technologies was not optimistic. The Technology Administration of the US Department of Commerce (1990) reported that as of 1989 the United States was losing badly – the Department of Commerce's worst of four categories – to Japan in advanced materials, biotechnology, digital-imaging technology, and superconductors. With respect to the Europeans, American firms were losing market share in digital-imaging technology and flexible integrated manufacturing, as shown in Table 9.3. The Council on Competitiveness (1991) reached a similar conclusion, noting that the United States was, at that time, experiencing declining market share in materials and associated processing technologies, engineering and production technologies, and electronic components. One response to the anticipated trends summarized in Table 9.3 was a policy effort to increase the speed with which

Table 9.3 Competitiveness of US industries in emerging technologies in the 1980s

Technology	United States versus Japan	United States versus European Community
Emerging materials (e.g. diamond think films, superconductors)	Significantly ahead in R&D and new products but losing competitiveness and expected to be behind by late 1980s	Moderately ahead in R&D and even in new products with no declining trend
Emerging electronics and information systems (e.g. advanced semiconductor devices, digital-imaging technologies, high-density data storage)	Moderately ahead in R&D but losing competitiveness and expected to be behind by early 1990s Significantly ahead in new products but losing competitiveness and expected to be behind by late 1980s	Moderately ahead in R&D and even in new products with no declining trend
Emerging manufacturing systems (e.g. artificial intelligence, flexible computer-integrated manufacturing, senson technology)	Significantly ahead in R&D but losing competitiveness but still expected to be ahead by end of 1990s Marginally ahead in new products with no declining trend	Moderately ahead in R&D with no declining trend Marginally ahead in new products but losing competitiveness and expected to be behind by end of 1980s
Emerging life sciences applications (e.g. biotechnology, medical devices, and diagnostics)	Significantly ahead in R&D but losing competitiveness but still expected to be ahead by end of 1990s Significantly ahead in new products but losing competitiveness and expected to be behind by early 1990s	Significantly ahead in R&D and gaining in competitiveness through 1990s Significantly ahead in new products but losing competitiveness and expected to be behind by end of 1990s

Source: US Department of Commerce (1990).

US firms could conduct their R&D. The R&E tax credit in 1981 was intended to affect the level of US R&D spending, but that emphasis was considered insufficient for increasing the pace of innovation at the time. The National Cooperative Research Act (NCRA) of 1984 created a process whereby firms could file research joint ventures with the US Department of Justice with a strong likelihood that the government would not prosecute them for engaging in collusive behavior.

While the overall effectiveness of this policy initiative is still somewhat unclear, Link and Bauer (1989) have shown that collaboration increases the efficiency with which firms conduct their in-house R&D. In terms of equation (9.9), they show that ρ is statistically greater among US manufacturing firms that engage in collaborative research than among those that do not. Hence, through collaboration, firms learn to conduct their R&D more efficiently and thus enjoy

78   *The technology–productivity growth relationship*

greater productivity growth and, according to Link and Bauer, greater competitive advantage. Link *et al.* (2002) have also shown that the NCRA is facilitating its goal of creating a favorable environment, or safe harbor, for the conduct of research cooperatively.

Infrastructure technologies are a second key source of technical knowledge. Few technologies developed through indigenous R&D can be successfully commercialized and achieve market penetration in the absence of infrastructure technologies. Following Tassey (1992) and Link and Tassey (1993), infrastructure technologies originate outside of the boundaries of the firm, as shown in Figure 8.2, and are accordingly elements of the technology base upon which all firms in the industry rely upon. These technologies include measurement methods, test methods, scientific and engineering databases used in the conduct of R&D, process controls, and various other standards. Infrastructure technologies increase the efficiency with which technology-based economic activity is conducted. They act collectively as a leveraging agent on R&D, as well as on production.

Most infrastructure technologies are in the public domain, especially those technologies created through research conducted in federal laboratories, as Leyden and Link (1992) have shown. However, the private sector also invests in infrastructure technology for important internal purposes such as to benchmark again national standards.

Using aggregated US manufacturing industry data, Link and Tassey (1993) showed that total factor productivity growth was greater in those industries where firms invest a larger portion of their self-financed R&D in infrastructure technology.

The science base resides in the public domain, but it is enriched primarily through basic research conducted at universities. Thus, university-based research is an important source of technical knowledge that, according to Figure 8.2, will leverage the efficiency with which firms conduct their R&D and hence will affect productivity growth. Findings from this literature were selectively noted under university spillovers in Table 8.4. More specific to the theme of this chapter, however, is the research by Link and Rees (1990). Referring to equation (9.9), Link and Rees showed, using a sample of US manufacturing firms, which could be divided into those involved with universities in research and those not, that the private rate of return to R&D, ρ in equation (9.9), was nearly three times as large for the group of firms with university research relationships.

10 Effects of information technology on workers and economic performance

As discussed in previous chapters, and especially with reference to both Figure 8.2 and equations (9.2) and (9.9), indigenous R&D entails a fundamental investment in the innovation process and one that drives productivity growth at all levels of aggregations. To a lesser extent, so too is purchased technology that enters the firm's production process in the form of new capital equipment. Such purchased technology embodies the innovations, and hence the R&D, of those firms producing new capital equipment.

Recall from equation (9.1), the generalizable production function applicable to the ith level of aggregation:

$$Q_i = A_i\, F(K, L, T)_i \qquad (10.1)$$

and recall the representation of T from equation (9.2) as:

$$T_i = G(OT_i, PT_i, GT_i, IT), \qquad (10.2)$$

where OT_i is the ith economic unit's own or self-financed stock of technical knowledge, PT_i is its purchased stock of technical knowledge, GT_i is its government-financed stock of technical knowledge, and IT is available infrastructure technology. Table 9.2 summarizes the foundation literature on the disaggregation of R&D; in this chapter we focus on the vast contemporary literature related to one particular purchased technology – information technology – and we do so within the context of a discussion of skill-biased technological change.

Skill-biased technological change

As discussed in Bound and Johnson (1992) and Petit and Soete (2001), a widening of the wage differential between low-skilled and high-skilled workers in almost all OECD nations has occurred despite a large increase in the number of high-skilled workers. One explanation for this increase in the rate of return to investment in education is what economists call skill-biased technological change (SBTC). The SBTC hypothesis, originally proposed by Nelson and Phelps (1966) and extended by Griliches (1969, 1970) and Welch (1970), asserts that the value of education is augmented by technological change because greater knowledge or skill enables firms to implement new technologies more effectively. Bartel and Lichtenberg (1987) contributed to this theoretical argument by asserting that the comparative advantage of highly skilled or highly educated workers in implementing new technologies arises from their ability to solve problems and adapt to change in the work environment. These theoretical models of SBTC predict, then, that technical change is biased, or non-neutral with respect to labor, having disproportionate effects on different classes of workers. In terms of the generalized production function that allows for non-neutral technical progress from equation (4.28):

$$Q = F(K, L, t) = G(a(t)K, b(t)L). \tag{10.3}$$

The SBTC literature assumes that technology augments labor productivity so that the relevant specification of equation (10.3) is:

$$Q = F(K, L, t) = G(K, b(t)L) \tag{10.4}$$

since $a(t) = 1$, which means that SBTC is Harrod neutral.

Determining whether technical change is non-neutral in the traditional Hicksian sense, or labor augmenting in the Harrod sense within the context of equation (10.4), is important in the productivity growth literature for several reasons. First, conventional measures of productivity growth are estimated under the Hicksian neutrality assumption. Imposing non-neutrality when this assumption is unwarranted could lead to biased and imprecise measures of productivity growth. Griliches (1996) noted that the earliest studies of the role of education in production were concerned with accounting for the high value of the Solow (1957) residual. His just concern was that unmeasured improvements in the quality of labor could lead to an underestimation of real labor input and thus to an overestimation of the true rate of growth in total factor productivity. That is why the growth-accounting studies discussed in previous chapters – in particular the studies by Jorgenson and Griliches (1967) and Jorgenson et al. (1987) – reported quality-adjusted measures of labor input based on indexes of workforce educational attainment.

Basic analytical framework

Many empirical studies of SBTC are based on the estimation of a cost function rather than a production function. Based on such a cost function, a wage equation is derived to examine the correlation between technological change and the productivity of labor, based on the maintained assumption that workers are paid their marginal products. More specifically, these models look at the relative cost or employment share devoted to skilled versus unskilled labor, or highly educated versus less educated labor.

In this regard, Berman et al. (1994) proposed the following labor cost (LC) function as:

$$LC_i = F(P_i, K, Q, t), \tag{10.5}$$

where P_i is the price or wage going to the ith category of worker, K is the stock of capital available to complement each category of worker, Q is output, and t indexes time. From an empirical perspective, most researchers assume two categories of workers, production (p) or non-skilled workers and non-production (np) or skilled workers, and that the functional form of the labor cost function, F( ), is translog. The use of only two types of employees is based on the simple fact that the statistical agencies in various countries – the Census Bureau in the United States – only collect information on these two classes of workers. Assuming the labor cost function, translog or otherwise, is homogeneous of degree one in prices and has constant returns to scale and homogeneity of degree one in prices, and taking first differences, Δ, yields a linear-in-logs relationship similar to:

$$\Delta s_{np} = \theta_1 \Delta \ln(P_{np}/P_p) + \theta_2 \Delta \ln(K/Q), \tag{10.6}$$

where s_{np} is the relative share of labor costs going to non-production workers, P_{np} is the price or wage of non-production workers, P_p is the price or wage of production workers. Empirically, if $\tau_2 > 0$ then, using Griliches' (1969) terminology, there is capital-skill complementarity.

Berman et al. (1994) extended the labor cost model in equation (10.5) by disaggregating the stock of capital, K, into the stock of R&D capital, R, and the stock of computer capital, C. If I represents the current flow of investment into K, then the Berman, Bound, and Griliches variation of equation (10.6) is:

$$\Delta s_{np} = \theta_1 \Delta \ln(P_{np}/P_p) + \theta_2 \Delta \ln(R/Q) + \theta_3 \Delta \ln(C/I). \tag{10.7}$$

Siegel (1999) extended this framework implied by equation (10.7) by making use of direct measures on the implementation of new technologies, rather than proxies for technological change, such as the rate of investment in R&D or computers. Specifically, he controlled for the average age of the firm's stock of advanced manufacturing technologies and the number of technologies employed by the company. Morrison and Siegel (2001) contributed to the SBTC literature by estimating a dynamic cost function, which allows the possibility that some inputs are fixed in the short run. They also added trade and outsourcing variables to this extended model and assessed the interaction between these factors and various technology indicators (R&D and computers).

Empirical studies of skill-biased technological change

Econometric issues aside, there is a vast literature on SBTC, with major contributions coming from scholars in various fields. This literature is summarized in detail in Table 10.1. Table 10.1 is more detailed than most of the previous tables since this body of literature is contemporary and most of the studies were published after the 1987 monograph.

Among other things, the table documents the alternative methodologies, data, and level of aggregation. However, the common theme is that each author reports

Table 10.1 Summary of empirical studies of skill-biased technological change

Author	Methodology	Country	Level of aggregation	Indicator of technical change	Measure of labor input	Findings
Dunne et al. (2000)	Regressions of non-production worker share on computers	US	Plant-level	Computer investment per worker	Non-production and production workers	Positive association between non-production worker share and computers, which appears to be growing over time; skill-biased technological change also appears to be associated with greater dispersion in wages and labor productivity over time
Morrison Paul and Siegel (2001)	Dynamic cost-function estimation with "high tech" capital	US	4-digit SIC industry-level	Computer capital and R&D	Four types of workers, classified by level of education	Computers and R&D reduce the demand for workers without a college degree and increase the demand for workers with at least some college. Trade has a strong indirect impact on the demand for less-educated workers, because it stimulates additional investment in computers
Bresnahan, et al. (2001)		US	Firm-level	Adoptions of 12 types of advanced manufacturing technologies (AMTs), which are grouped into two classes: "linked" versus integrated AMTs	Six classes of workers (managerial and supervisory, technical and professional, R&D, clerical and administrative, direct labor and supporting personnel, and other)	Technology adoption is associated with shifts in labor composition in favor of highly educated workers and greater employee empowerment; the magnitudes of the skill-bias and empowerment effects may depend on the type of technology that is implemented
Siegel (1999)	Regressions of levels and changes in employment shares (for 6 classes of workers) on dummy variables for technology adoption	US	Firm-level			

Bartel and Sicherman (1999)	Estimation of wage equations	US	Worker data (NLSY) matched to industry-level data	Expenditures on computers, R&D	Non-production and production workers	Positive correlation between wages and proxies for technical change, which is stronger for non-production workers than for production workers; the wage premium is attributed to the greater demand for ability in industries experiencing technical change
Haskel (1999)	Regressions of changes in relative wages of skilled and unskilled workers on computers	UK	3-digit SIC industry-level	Dummy variable denoting whether a plant introduced new equipment based on microchip technology	Skilled and unskilled workers	Positive correlation between relative wages and computers; wage premium for skill rose by 13% in the 1980s in the UK; computers account for about half of this increase
Haskel and Heden (1999)	Regressions of changes in wage-bill share for four classes of workers on computers and R&D	UK	Plant- and industry-level	Expenditures on computers, R&D	Proportion of firms in sector using computers in production process; non-manual and manual workers split into skilled and unskilled categories	Positive correlation between the relative wages of skilled non-manual workers and computers (also R&D); computerization reduces the demand for manual workers (both skilled and unskilled workers)
Berman et al. (1998)	Cross-country correlations of within-industry changes in the proportion of non-production workers	9 OECD countries	2- and 3-digit SIC industries	Expenditures on computers, R&D	Employment and wage shares for production and non-production workers	Positive correlation across 9 OECD countries in within industry changes in shares of non-production workers

(Continued)

Table 10.1 (Continued)

Author	Methodology	Country	Level of aggregation	Indicator of technical change	Measure of labor input	Findings
Autor et al. (1998)	Estimation of wage equations	US	Worker data (CPS)	Dummy variable denoting whether a worker uses a computer	Detailed data on workers: age, sex, race, union status, region	Workers who use a computer at work earn a 17–20% wage premium; computers could account for 30–50% of the recent increase in demand for highly skilled workers
Hildreth (1998)	Estimation of wage equations	UK	Data on workers and plants that employ them	Dummy variable denoting whether a plant invested in a new product or process technology	No data on labor composition	Workers employed at plants that invest in new process technologies earn higher wages; rent sharing (between workers and firms) is strongest in high-tech plants
Siegel (1997)	Regressions of an index of labor quality on the rate of investment in computers	US	4-digit SIC industry-level	Expenditures on computers, R&D	Non-production and production workers	Positive correlation between indicators of labor quality and investments in computers
Doms et al. (1997)	Estimation of wage equations	US	Data on workers and plants that employ them	Plant-level data on adoptions of advanced manufacturing technologies	Occupational mix, education	Positive correlation between technology usage and levels of but not changes in wages, skill, and education
Betts (1997)	Estimation of a translog cost function	Canada	Industry-level	Time	Non-production and production workers	Strong evidence of biased technical change away from blue-collar workers
Dinardo and Pischke (1997)	Estimation of wage equations	Germany	Worker data matched to industry-level data	Dummies for whether a worker sits down, uses a telephone, calculator, pen and pencil	Detailed data on workers: age, sex, race, union status, region	Workers who use a computer earn a wage premium, but so do those who sit down while they work or use a calculator, telephone, pen and pencil

Study	Methodology	Country	Level	Technology measure	Labor measure	Findings
Dunne et al. (1996)	Regressions of changes in non-production workers' shares in employment on R&D and the number of advanced manufacturing technologies adopted	US	Plant-level	Firm-level measures of R&D; plant-level measures of adoptions of advanced manufacturing technologies	Non-production and production workers	Positive correlation between changes in non-production labor share and technology usage
Machin (1996)	Regressions of changes in skilled workers' share in employment on various proxies for technological change	UK	Industry- and plant-levels	R&D intensity, innovation counts, introduction of microcomputers	Industry-level: manual and non-manual workers; plant-level: employment shares for 6 skill groups	Positive correlation between changes in non-manual labor share and R&D and innovations; skill upgrading associated with computers only for workers with highest level of skill
Park (1996)	Regressions of changes in relative wages of skilled and unskilled workers on computers	Korea	2-digit SIC industry-level	Growth in labor productivity	All workers, excluding unskilled	Positive correlation between labor productivity growth and the proportion of multiskilled workers in Korean manufacturing
Van Reenen (1996)	Estimation of wage equations with panel data on innovations	UK	Firm-level	Number of firm innovations and patents granted	No data on labor composition	Innovative firms pay above-average wages
Chennells and Van Reenen (1995)	Estimation of wage equations	UK	Plant-level	Plant-level data on technology usage	3 classes of workers: skilled, semi-skilled, unskilled	Positive correlation between technology usage and wages
Dunne and Schmitz (1995)	Regressions of changes in relative wages of skilled and unskilled workers on computers	US	Plant-level	Plant-level data on adoptions of advanced manufacturing technologies	Non-production and production workers	Plants with a high rate of technology adoption pay higher wages and employ a larger percentage of non-production workers

(Continued)

Table 10.1 (Continued)

Author	Methodology	Country	Level of aggregation	Indicator of technical change	Measure of labor input	Findings
Entorf and Kramarz (1995)	Estimation of wage equations	France	Data on workers and firms that employ them	Firm-level data on usage of 3 computer-based technologies	Occupational mix: unskilled and skilled blue-collar, clerks, managers, engineers, professionals	Positive correlation between technology usage and wages; highest wage premiums earned by those with the lowest level of skill
Regev (1995)	Estimation of production function	Israel	Firm-level	Technology index based on quality of labor and capital and R&D investment	No decomposition of labor	Technology-intensive firms pay higher average wages, generated new jobs during a period of downsizing
Reilly (1995)	Estimation of wage equations	Canada	Data on workers and plants that employ them	Dummy variable denoting whether a firm has access to computers	Detailed data on workers: occupation, industry, age, tenure, region, experience	Workers that have access to computers earn a 13% wage premium
Berman et al. (1994)	Regressions of changes in relative wages of skilled and unskilled workers on computers	US	4-digit SIC industry-level	Expenditures on computers, R&D	Employment and wage shares for non-production and production workers	Positive correlation between computers and R&D and changes in production workers' share in employment and wages
Mishel and Bernstein (1994)	Regressions of changes in relative wages of skilled and unskilled workers on computers	US	2-digit SIC industry-level	Computer equipment capital per worker, employment share of scientists and engineers	Education, gross and residual wage inequality	Positive association between technology proxies and proportion of educated labor, but not stronger in the 1980s than in the 1970s

Study	Method	Country	Data level	Variables used to measure technology	Skill definition	Main finding
Krueger (1993)	Estimation of wage equations	US	Worker, CPS	Dummy variable denoting whether a worker uses a computer	Detailed data on workers: 8 occupations, age, sex, union status	Workers who use a computer at work earn a 10–15% wage premium
Berndt et al. (1992)	Regressions of changes in relative wages of skilled and unskilled workers on computers	US	2-digit SIC industry-level	Computer capital	Age, education cells for non-production and production workers	Positive correlation between share of high-tech office equipment and employment share of non-production workers
Bartel and Lichtenberg (1990)	Estimation of wage equations	US	Workers in 3-digit SIC industries	Proxies for age of the capital stock, R&D	Age, education, sex	Inverse relationship between the age of technology and wages of highly educated workers
Lynch and Osterman (1989)	Estimation of labor demand curves for 10 occupational classes of workers	US	Firm-level (n = 1), telephone company	Technical change in switching equipment, production of operators, capital expenditures	10 occupational classes of workers	Innovation favors professional employees, also leads to greater centralization
Bartel and Lichtenberg (1987)	Estimation of restricted (variable) labor cost function	US	3-digit SIC industry-level	Proxies for age of the capital stock	Age, education, sex	Inverse relationship between technology and the percentage of labor cost devoted to highly educated workers
Osterman (1986)	Regressions of changes in relative wages of skilled and unskilled workers on computers	US	2-digit SIC industry-level	Industry measure of total computer memory	Several occupational classes: clerks, non-data-entry clerks, and managers	Computerization reduces employment of clerks and managers, not as much for managers in the long run

evidence that is consistent with some aspect of the theory of skill-biased technical change. That is, the literature clearly shows that technological change – be it coming from R&D or embodied in computers or other advanced manufacturing technologies – is positively correlated with wages and, more importantly, with shifts in labor composition in favor of production or skilled workers versus non-production or less-skilled workers.

Many studies report findings based on industry-level regressions of changes in employment shares or wages on proxies for technological change, such as R&D investment. For example, Berman *et al.* (1994) reported a positive association between investment in computers and R&D and changes in non-production workers' share of the industry wage bill in US manufacturing industries, which they interpret as indicative of skill upgrading. Based on similar techniques, Mishel and Bernstein (1994) included the employment share of scientists and engineers in the industry as an additional indicator of technological change. They also found a positive correlation between proxies for technological change and shifts in demand in favor of highly educated workers. However, they reported that the strength of this association has not become stronger in the 1980s.

Other industry-level studies have been consistent with these results. Berndt *et al.* (1992) reported a positive correlation between high-technology office equipment and the demand for white-collar workers. In a more recent study, based on estimation of a latent variables model, Siegel (1997) found a positive association between proxies for labor quality and computer investment for US manufacturing industries. Finally, Bartel and Lichtenberg (1987, 1990) reported that the demand for highly educated workers is inversely related to the age of an industry's technology. This finding is consistent with the authors' theoretical model that the demand for learning is highest when the firm implements a new technology. Consistent with such so-called efficiency wage models, Bartel and Lichtenberg argued that a higher wage is also needed to elicit higher levels of effort in the aftermath of technological change.

An analysis of industry-level data from foreign countries has yielded similar patterns. Berman *et al.* (1998) determined that changes in the employment structure in favor of highly educated workers are evident across many developed countries. The authors concluded that these wage and employment shifts can be linked to technological change. Also, the magnitudes of these linkages are quite similar across countries. Additional international evidence has been provided by Park (1996), who reported a positive correlation between labor productivity growth and the proportion of multi-skilled workers in Korean manufacturing industries. For two-digit manufacturing industries in Canada, Betts (1997) estimated a fully specified translog cost function model with a time trend, a proxy for technical change, as an additional argument. He found evidence of non-neutral Hicksian technical change over time away from blue-collar labor in the majority of the industries he studied.

The SBTC studies conducted by labor economists, as opposed to industrial organization or production/technology economists, have tended to focus on the wage and employment implications of SBTC. Examples of those who have followed this approach include Mincer (1989), Davis and Haltiwanger (1991), Levy and Murnane (1997), Katz and Murphy (1992), Murphy and Welch (1989, 1992), Juhn *et al*. (1993), and Autor *et al*. (1996). Their research has successfully attempted to determine how much of the increase in wage inequality between skilled and non-skilled workers, and how much of the concomitant increase in the demand for skilled and more highly educated workers can be attributed to the use of new technologies. Davis and Haltiwanger (1991) documented a large increase in the 1980s in the earnings differential between non-production and production worker wages. The authors attributed these changes to labor-augmenting technical change, which had increased the relative demand of the more highly skilled and educated workers.

The first major study to link changes in the wage structure at the individual level to technology usage was by Krueger (1993). Krueger reported, from his analysis of US Bureau of Labor Statistics data, that workers who use computers on the job earned in the 1980s a wage premium of 10 percent to 15 percent relative to observationally equivalent workers. Reilly (1995) found that Canadian workers with access to computers earned a 13 percent wage premium during an earlier period. Autor *et al*. (1998) updated Krueger's (1993) earlier study, showing that the wage premium has increased in the last decade to approximately 17 percent. More importantly, the authors concluded that investments in computers could account for as much as 35 percent to 50 percent of the increase in the growth in demand for more highly skilled workers.

There have also been several firm and plant-level studies of skill-biased technical change in the United States, France, and the United Kingdom. Many argue that industry-level studies of SBTC could be subject to aggregation biases, much like the case of production-function studies are more aggregated levels. As with the impact of technology on production, it is more desirable to examine the impact of technology on wages and labor composition at the plant or firm level because there could be substantial variation in these effects within industries. The first firm-level study was conducted by Lynch and Osterman (1989), who estimated labor demand curves for workers employed by a single firm in the telecommunications industry. The authors reported that technological innovations stimulated an increase in the demand for technical and professional workers.

Using microeconomic data at the plant level, Siegel (1999) found that the implementation of a new technology leads to downsizing and a shift in labor composition and compensation in favor of white-collar workers. More importantly, he showed that there is considerable heterogeneity in downsizing and skill-upgrading across different classes of technologies, thus concluding that the magnitude of the skill-bias may depend on the type of technology that is implemented.

A cross-sectional, plant-level study was also conducted by Dunne and Schmitz (1995). The authors reported that technology-intensive plants pay higher wages than less-technology-intensive plants within the same industry.

Evidence from labor markets in the United Kingdom and Israel is consistent with this finding. Van Reenen (1996) examined panel data on wages and innovation for a sample of British firms whose shares were publicly traded for at least five years between 1976 and 1982. Controlling for the endogeneity of innovations, he concluded that innovative firms pay above average wages. Regev (1998) estimated a simple production-function model for a panel dataset of Israeli firms. He constructed a technology index for each firm consisting of measures of the quality of labor, capital, and R&D investment. The author reported that technology-intensive firms pay above-average wages and are consistently more productive than other firms in the same industry. He also found that these firms demonstrated net job creation during a period when many companies were downsizing.

One of the most important developments in empirical analysis of skill-biased technological change has been the creation of data sets that match workers to their place of employment. Traditional studies of the labor supply behavior of individuals have suffered from limited information regarding the demand for a worker's labor. To understand the nature of this demand, and to help sort out the determinants of intra- and inter-industry wage differentials, it is helpful to simultaneously explore data on the characteristics of workers and firms. Note that conventional US-based data sets used in labor market studies, such as the Current Population Survey, the National Longitudinal Survey (NLS), or the Panel Study of Income Dynamics (PSID), do not have detailed information on the employer.

Researchers at the US Census Bureau have constructed the Worker-Establishment Characteristic Database (WECD), a file that links detailed demographic data from the 1990 Decennial Census to comprehensive information on plants contained in the Longitudinal Research Database (LRD). See Troske (1994). The LRD is a compilation of data on establishments from the Census of Manufacturers (CM) and the Annual Survey of Manufacturers (ASM). This file has also been linked to the SMT, which provides detailed information on advanced manufacturing technology usage. There are now two cross-sections of the SMT, a 1988 and a 1993 version.

The linked version of the WECD and SMT has been analyzed by Dunne *et al.* (1996) and Doms *et al.* (1997). Both studies reported a positive correlation between technology usage and levels, but not changes, in wages and education. The authors also concluded that high-wage, high-skill plants are more likely to adopt new technologies. They found no evidence of workforce adjustment or skill-upgrading in the aftermath of technology adoption. While the cross-sectional analysis of wage and compositional effects is much richer than the previous Census study, conducted by Dunne and Schmitz (1995), the longitudinal analysis suffered from two important limitations. The first is that they can only measure changes in employment and wages for two types of employees: production and non-production workers. Second, they cannot identify the year of technology adoption, which precludes a precise analysis of timing effects.

Matched employee–employer data sets have also been constructed in England and France. Chennells and van Reenen (1995) examined the 1984 Workplace Industrial Relations Survey (WIRS), a plant-level survey conducted in the United Kingdom. Using this data set, the authors found that the skill categories of skilled, semi-skilled, unskilled, and clerical received wages commensurate with the technology that they used. Chennels and van Reenen found a technology usage wage premium of about 5 percent for skilled workers and about 10 percent for semi-skilled and unskilled workers. Overall, the technology wage premium was about 7 percent.

Machin (1996) linked the WIRS survey to the SPRU innovation database. This effort enabled him to construct two additional proxies for technological change: R&D intensity and innovation counts, and he found that R&D and innovations are positively associated with shifts in labor composition in favor of more highly educated workers. However, computers are associated with skill upgrading only for workers with the highest level of education or skill.

Entorf and Kramarz (1995) examined a French matched employee–employer panel dataset with detailed measures of labor composition and technology usage. The authors also found a positive correlation between technology usage and wages. Interestingly, they found the highest wage premiums accrue to workers with the lowest level of skill. It is interesting to note that both Chennells and van Reenen (1995) and Entorf and Kramarz (1995) concluded that it is unlikely that the usage of new technology caused higher wages, casting doubt on the conventional interpretation of the wage premium on computers or new technology as reflecting a true return to the worker on the firm's investment in technology. Rather, their interpretation of their findings were that for many highly educated and skilled workers, proficiency with a new technology is expected, and thus, already factored into the current wage. See also Dinardo and Pischke (1997). Of course, it is difficult to sort out these issues without more precise information on the timing of innovations.

Finally, as noted earlier, Morrison Paul and Siegel (2001) added to the SBTC literature by estimating a dynamic, flexible cost function using US manufacturing industry data. The authors reported that technology has a stronger impact on shifts in labor composition in favor of highly educated workers than trade or outsourcing. The effects of computers and R&D do not appear to differ substantially. Trade also had a negative impact on the demand for less educated workers, but it is not associated with an increase in demand for more educated workers. Outsourcing appears to have a relatively small negative impact on demand across all education levels, with the strongest effects for workers with less than a college degree. Perhaps their most interesting result concerns the interaction between trade and computers. Specifically, they found that trade induces computerization, which exacerbates the negative impact that each factor has on the demand for workers without a college degree, and augments the positive effects that each factor has on the demand for workers with a college degree. Thus, models that ignore these indirect effects could underestimate the overall impact of trade on labor composition.

Empirical studies of the impact of computers on economic performance

There is also a burgeoning empirical literature on the relationship between computers and productivity. Part of the interest in this topic has been sparked by Solow's famous quip to the effect that computers show up everywhere except in the productivity statistics. That comment has become known as the Solow productivity paradox.

A summary of some recent empirical studies is presented in Table 10.2. Note that, in contrast to the SBTC literature, most articles analyze US data. However, authors have conducted such studies at all levels of aggregation ranging from the plant to the nation. Many studies have offered econometric estimates based on a Cobb–Douglas production function, with an additional variable serving as a proxy for investment in computer capital, as opposed to conventional physical capital. This type of specification parallels that in equation (10.1) where T is the stock of technical capital as proxied by investments in computer capital. Other authors, such as Lichtenberg (1995) and Brynjolfsson and Hitt (1996) have also calculated estimates of computer labor. Much of that firm-level evidence suggests that there are excess (firm-level) returns to computer labor (marginal products that vastly exceed wages), suggesting that Solow might have been premature in his prediction.

However, in contrast to the SBTC studies, there was a lack of a consensus regarding empirical results, at least in some of the early studies. At the aggregate level, Oliner and Sichel (1994) found that computers did not make a significant contribution to output growth. Using industry-level data, Catherine Morrison (1997) reached a similar conclusion. Berndt et al. (1992) estimated industry-level production functions and found that investments in computers are uncorrelated with total factor productivity growth in most industries. Parsons et al. (1993) reported very low marginal rates of returns on investments in computers for Canadian banks. On the other hand, Siegel and Griliches (1992) found a positive and statistically significant relationship between a manufacturing industry's rate of investment in computers and its total factor productivity growth. At the firm level, Lichtenberg (1995) estimated production functions and, as referenced earlier, found strong evidence of excess returns to information-systems equipment and labor.

Siegel (1997) provided a direct test of Solow's hypothesis by attempting to control for measurement error that arises in the aftermath of investments in computers and R&D. Specifically, he estimated the standard model outlined in equation (9.9), adding an additional term reflecting the rate of investment in computers:

$$A'/A = \lambda + \rho_1 (R\Delta/Q) + \rho_2 (C/Q) \tag{10.8}$$

More importantly, however, he estimated this equation in the context of a full errors-in-variables model, allowing for the possibility that all inputs and output are measured with error. The author hypothesized that investments in computers exacerbate errors in measuring output and input prices because computers improve output and labor quality. As noted in previous chapters, these improvements are not properly accounted for in conventional productivity statistics, which results in estimates of the returns to computers that have a downward bias. Based on industry-level data, he found that the empirical evidence is consistent with this hypothesis. More importantly, when adjustments are made for measurement errors, computers do, in fact, enhance productivity growth.

Table 10.2 Summary of empirical studies of the relationship between computers and productivity growth

Author	Methodology	Country/Sector	Level of aggregation	Findings
Dunne et al. (2000)	Regressions of labor productivity on computers	US/manufacturing	Plant-level	Positive association between computers and labor productivity, which appears to be growing over time
McGuckin and Stiroh (1999)	Cobb–Douglas production function with computer capital	US/manufacturing and service	Aggregate, major sector, and 2-digit SIC industry-levels	Evidence of excess returns capital at each level of aggregation
Lehr and Lichtenberg (1999)	Cobb–Douglas production function with computer capital and labor	US/manufacturing and service	Firm-level	Excess returns to computer capital, especially personal computers. The returns to computers appear to have peaked in 1986 or 1987
Wolff (1999)	Regressions of non-parametric measures of total factor productivity growth (constructed from input–output tables) on investment in computers	US/manufacturing and service	Industry-level (85 sectors)	No evidence of a positive relationship between computers and productivity growth. Weak evidence of a positive association in goods industries during 1977–87
Licht and Moch (1999)	Cobb–Douglas production function including three types of computers (terminals, UNIX workstations, and PCs)	Germany/manufacturing and service	Firm-level	Terminals have a positive impact on productivity in goods industries, but not in services. Strong positive relationship between PCs and productivity in manufacturing and services
Gera et al. (1999)	Cobb–Douglas production function with computer capital	US and Canada/manufacturing	Industry-level	Positive correlation between investment in computers and labor productivity growth
Stolarick (1999)	Cobb–Douglas production function with computer capital	US/manufacturing	Plant-level	Positive relationship between spending on computers and plant productivity
Bharadwaj et al. (1999)	Regressions of Tobin's q on measures of investment in information technology	US/manufacturing and service	Firm-level	Positive association between investments in information technology and Tobin's q

(Continued)

Table 10.2 (Continued)

Author	Methodology	Country/Sector	Level of aggregation	Findings
McGuckin et al. (1998)	Regressions of labor productivity on dummies denoting whether the plant uses a computer-based manufacturing technology	US/manufacturing and service	Plant-level	Plants using advanced computer-based technologies have higher levels of productivity; weaker evidence on the relationship between technology usage and productivity growth
Lehr and Lichtenberg (1998)	Cobb–Douglas production function with computer capital and labor	US/public sector	Organizational level (government agencies)	Excess returns to computer capital
Stiroh (1998)	Sectoral growth accounting methods and regression analysis based on a Cobb–Douglas production function	US/manufacturing and service	2-digit SIC industry-level	The sector that produces computers (SIC 35) has made a strong contribution to economic growth; computer-using sectors have not made a similar contribution. No evidence of a positive relationship between computers and total factor productivity growth at the sectoral level
Siegel (1997)	Latent variables model: regressions of parametric and non-parametric measures of total factor productivity growth on the rate of investment in computers	US/manufacturing 4-digit SIC	Industry-level	When controls are included in the model for measurement errors, computers have a positive and statistically significant impact on productivity
Morrison (1997)	Use of a dynamic cost function to calculate Tobin's q benefit/cost ratios for high-tech capital	US/manufacturing	2-digit SIC industry-level	There are positive returns to computers. However, there is over-investment in computers, given that the benefit/cost ratio <1 for most of the time period
Morrison and Siegel (1997)	Dynamic cost function estimation with "high-tech" capital	US/manufacturing	4-digit SIC industry-level	External investments in computers by related industries (4-digit industries within a 2-digit sector) enhance productivity
Greenan and Mairesse (1996)	Cobb–Douglas production function with computer capital	France/manufacturing and service	Firm-level	Impact of computers is positive and at least as large as for other types of capital. Returns appear to be higher in services than in manufacturing
Brynjolfsson and Hitt (1996)	Cobb–Douglas production function with computer capital and labor	US/manufacturing and service	Firm-level	Excess returns to computer capital and labor

Study	Method	Country/Sector	Level	Findings
Hitt and Brynjolfsson (1996)	Cobb–Douglas production function with computer capital and labor	US/manufacturing and service	Firm-level	Computers enhance productivity and consumer surplus, but not profitability
Lichtenberg (1995)	Cobb–Douglas production function with computer capital and labor	US/manufacturing and service	Firm-level	Excess returns to computer capital and labor
Berndt and Morrison (1995)	Cobb–Douglas production function with "high-tech" capital	US/manufacturing	2-digit SIC industry-level	Increases in the share of high-tech capital were, at best, uncorrelated with total factor productivity
Jorgenson and Stiroh (1995)	Sectoral growth accounting methods	US	Aggregate-level	Computer equipment has made a very small contribution to economic growth (roughly the same estimate as Oliner and Sichel (1994))
Oliner and Sichel (1994)	Growth-accounting methods used to estimate the contribution of computers to economic growth	US	Aggregate-level	Under standard neoclassical assumptions, computers account for only a small percentage (0.15%) of average annual economic growth
Jorgenson and Stiroh (2000)	Sectoral growth-accounting methods	US	Aggregate-level	The growth contribution of computers increased substantially in the mid-to-late 1990s
Parsons et al. (1993)	Estimation of a translog cost function with computer capital	Canada/service	Industry-level	Very low returns on investments in computers for banks
Loveman (1993)	Estimation of a Cobb–Douglas production function	US/manufacturing and service	Business-unit level	Output elasticity estimates for computers insignificantly different from zero (marginal product of computers is zero); recent empirical studies of the relationship between computers and productivity
Siegel and Griliches (1992)	Correlation between non-parametric measures of total factor productivity and rate of investment in computers	US/manufacturing	4-digit SIC industry-level	Positive correlation between rate of investment in computers and total factor productivity growth
Lau and Tokutsu (1992)	Cost-function estimation to impute production function parameters	US	Aggregate-level	The authors attribute 50% of the growth in real output over the past three decades to growth in computer capital
Steindel (1992)	Cobb–Douglas production function with "high-tech" capital	US/manufacturing	2-digit SIC industry-level	Industries with higher rates of investment in computers experienced higher growth in productivity

Table 10.3 Sources of economic growth and computers, 1959–98

Composition of growth	1959–73	1973–90	1990–98
Output growth	4.32	3.13	3.44
Contribution of capital (K)	1.41	1.15	1.07
Non-computer capital	1.31	0.92	0.68
Computers and software	0.10	0.24	0.39
Contribution of consumers' Durables services (D)	0.62	0.47	0.35
Non-computer capital	0.62	0.45	0.25
Computers and software	0.00	0.02	0.10
Contribution of labor (L)	1.25	1.17	1.32
Aggregate total factor productivity	1.05	0.34	0.70

Source: Jorgenson and Stiroh (2000).

Morrison and Siegel (1997) extended the simple Cobb–Douglas production framework implicit in equation (10.8) by also estimating a dynamic, flexible cost function at the industry level. Theirs is also the first study to consider the effect of external investments in computers on the productivity of a given industry, where external refers to computer investments undertaken by other four-digit SIC industries within the same two-digit industry group. The authors found strong evidence of spillover effects, namely that an increase in external investments in R&D and computers have a positive effect on productivity.

Stiroh (2001) and Jorgenson and Stiroh (2000) reported a positive finding regarding the aggregate impact of investment in information technology. In earlier work, Jorgenson and Stiroh (1995) found that computers made only a very small contribution to economic growth, reporting estimates that were quite similar to those presented in Oliner and Sichel (1994). Jorgenson and Stiroh (2000) concluded that the impact of information technology on the overall economy had been increasing over time. Their findings, which are presented in Table 10.3, indicated that computer hardware and software accounted for a much greater fraction of economic growth in the 1990s than in previous periods. Note, however, that non-computer capital, R&D-based in particular, is still by far more important as a source of economic growth than computer capital.

Technological change, organizational change, and economic performance

Economists have only recently become interested in the subject of organizational change, in part because they have been somewhat reluctant to go inside the so-called black box and examine managerial practices. Although there has been some recent theoretical work on organizational design and managerial practices by, for example, Athey and Stern (1998) and Milgrom and Roberts (1990), there have been few studies of the relationship between technological change, organizational practices, worker skill, and economic performance.

Effects of IT on workers and economic performance 97

However, scholars who have analyzed the impact of information technology on worker or firm performance have in recent years come to realize that the use of information technology is often accompanied by dramatic changes in the work environment. Siegel (1999) and Bresnahan *et al.* (2001) pioneered this literature. At the firm level, Siegel (1999) found that the implementation of new technologies resulted in companies investing additional resources in training and also led to enhanced employee empowerment. Based on supplemental case studies and field visits (to the firms who completed his survey), the author concluded that organizational change often accompanied technological change. These organizational changes were sometimes quite dramatic, mainly because many of the technologies that were implemented by the companies were integrative and thus had a major impact on numerous functional areas of the firm including R&D, marketing, purchasing, logistics, manufacturing, and materials management. More importantly, the newly introduced technologies changed the work environment. That is, in the aftermath of the adoption of a new technology, information, and other duties that were previously departmentalized or compartmentalized were shared among workers performing different functional tasks.

Bresnahan *et al.* (2001) also provided evidence on the relationship between technological change, organizational change, and performance. The authors hypothesized that decentralized decision-making and greater communication within an organization are required to implement new technologies successfully, and their estimates confirmed that the interaction of computer capital and managerial decentralization is strongly positive. They also showed that decentralized firms generate a higher marginal return on their investments in computers.

These are areas of research that will long occupy the research agenda of academics, especially academics who cross functional boundaries in an effort to understand the complexity of the relationship between technological change and economic performance.

11 Research partnerships and economic performance

The emergence of new organizational forms

Recent decades have witnessed the emergence and widespread growth of new organizational forms to conduct R&D, which we refer to as research partnerships. These partnerships involve firms, universities, non-profit organizations, and public agencies. The growth in such alliances can be attributed to the expansion of public–private partnerships, relaxation of antitrust enforcement to promote collaborative research, policies designed to stimulate more rapid diffusion of technologies from universities to firms, and growth in venture-capital investment in high technology start-ups. These alliances constitute potential sources of R&D spillovers and economic growth, as illustrated in Figure 8.2 and in Table 8.4, and thus, have important policy implications.

Examples of research partnerships in the United States are research joint ventures (RJVs), strategic alliances, strategic networks, industry consortia, cooperative research and development agreements (CRADAs) between federal laboratories and firms, National Science Foundation-sponsored Engineering Research Centers (ERCs) and industry–university cooperative research centers (IUCRCs), federally funded research and development centers (FFRDCs). These alliances also include various dimensions of university technology transfer, such as licensing and sponsored research agreements, science parks, university-based entrepreneurial start-ups, co-authoring between academics and industry scientists, faculty consulting, and educational partnerships involving universities and firms.

Note that by example we have defined research partnerships quite broadly. Some of each type of these alliances have gained in prominence in the new economy, with its greater emphasis on intellectual property, venture capital, entrepreneurial start-ups, and university–industry technology transfer (UITT). As described in Siegel *et al.* (1999), the recent increase in UITT, through a university technology transfer office (TTO) and other formal means, has led to a concomitant increase in the incidence and complexity of research partnerships involving universities and firms. The authors also reported that universities have become much more receptive to the idea of accepting an equity position in an entrepreneurial start-up, in lieu of up-front licensing revenue, thus signaling that the boundaries of university activity are expanding.

The two categories of research partnerships, faculty consulting and educational partnerships involving universities and firms, constitute informal means of transferring technologies from universities to firms. According to a recent National Academy of Engineering (NAE) study, summarized by Grossman et al. (2001), these research partnerships may also be important determinants of technological spillovers. The NAE study examined the contributions of academic research to industrial performance in five major industries and concluded that in some sectors, faculty consulting and educational partnerships between universities and firms played a critical role in the introduction of new production processes.

Private–private research partnerships versus public–private research partnerships

It is important to distinguish between private–private research partnerships and public–private research partnerships. Most research partnerships fall into the latter category. Public–private research partnerships, by definition, receive some level of support from a public institution. Such support can assume various forms, such as government subsidies for projects funded by private firms, shared use of expertise and laboratory facilities, university technology incubators, science parks, licensing agreements between universities and firms, and university-based start-ups. Private–private research partnerships are defined as relationships involving only firms such as research joint ventures, strategic alliances, and networks involving two or more firms.

Despite the ubiquity of research partnerships and their potential importance as a mechanism for generating technological spillovers, it is difficult to evaluate the impact of these partnerships on economic performance, given the limitations of existing data. That is unfortunate because an assessment of the desirability of these policy initiatives ultimately depends on scholars' ability to derive accurate estimates of the private and social returns associated with such partnerships, public–private partnerships in particular. Data limitations aside, performance should be conceptualized in terms of overcoming market failures as Link and Scott (1998) and Martin and Scott (2000) have argued. In practice, however, some use a performance indicator of a public–private partnership that captures how the partnership has increased the productivity of the region or industry, job or new firm creation, or some proxy for technological spillovers.

Of course, the relevant metric of performance for a private–private research partnership will be some measure of the private returns to the firms involved in the partnerships. Such metrics could be enhanced profitability, productivity growth, increases in market share, or increases in the firm's share price, if the firm's stock is publicly traded.

We assume that for private–private partnerships, the key objective for a firm to enter into such an arrangement is profit, or some activity that will eventually generate profits. Hence, scholars who examine such relationships tend to focus on the impact of research partnerships on stock prices or accounting profits, but an equally valid area of inquiry could be the impact of research partnerships on enhanced innovative activity, which over time would lead to higher profits.

Thus, from a public policy perspective, once appropriate antitrust and intellectual property laws have been designed, public–private research partnerships are likely to be of greater interest than collaborations involving firms only. In theory, they should generate technological spillovers and ultimately, high social returns. If research partnerships are achieving their goals, one would expect to see a reduction over time in the magnitudes of the market failures they address.

An assessment of the performance of private–private research partnerships is of less policy interest since public moneys are not at stake unless it can be shown that market failures are inhibiting the formation of such alliances.

Another interesting policy issue involving public–private research partnerships is the trend towards greater scrutiny of public investments in R&D. As described in Link and Scott (1998), this stems, in part, from recent initiatives to hold public technology-based institutions more accountable for documenting the economic impact of the R&D projects they have supported. Universities, public as well as private, face similar pressures from the legislative bodies that provide funding. In contrast, for private–private partnerships, shareholder accountability has always been a powerful force in constraining self-serving behavior on the part of corporate managers, ensuring that they will closely monitor the financial return on investment in research partnerships.

Overview of empirical studies: the impact of research partnerships on economic performance

Table 11.1 summarizes the key features of recent studies of research partnerships and economic performance. For each study, we denote the type of research partnership, nature of the institutions involved in the research partnership, unit of observation, data sets used in the empirical analysis, methodology, and proxies for performance. Note that scholars in a wide variety of disciplines, such as economics, finance, sociology, public policy, and strategic management have examined research partnerships.

Interdisciplinary interest in this topic offers several advantages, including an increase in the number of data sets available to researchers, consideration of research partnerships in specific industries and nations, a broader understanding of the antecedents and consequences of these relationships, and the use of numerous indicators of performance, since notions of performance vary substantially across fields. Consider each of these in turn.

Three major data sets analyzed in these studies are the MERIT–CATI (Maastricht Economic Research Institute on Innovation and Technology – Cooperative Agreements and Technology Indicators) file, NSF's CORE (COoperative REsearch) database, and the NCRA–RJV (National Cooperative Research Act – Research Joint Venture) database. Hagedoorn *et al.* (2000) discuss these databases in detail. Many authors have examined special data sets consisting of firms that have received funds from government programs that support technology-based research partnerships, such as the US Department of Commerce's Advanced Technology Program and Small Business Innovation

Research (SBIR) programs. Typically, these authors then link this information to firm-level surveys of production, R&D, accounting profitability, and stock prices in order to assess the impact of the research partnerships on economic or financial performance.

The extant literature on research partnerships reflects a mix of quantitative and qualitative research methods. In fact, some researchers have designed their own surveys of firms involved in research partnerships, typically with government or foundation support. More importantly, numerous authors have made liberal use of proprietary databases. Studies examining research partnerships resulting from university–industry technology transfer have been based on the comprehensive survey conducted by the Association of University Technology Managers (AUTM), as well as archival data on patents, licenses, and start-ups at several major universities. Several other authors, especially in the field of strategic management, have collected data on specific industries, such as chemicals, biotechnology, and semiconductors.

Table 11.1 also reveals that authors have used a wide variety of performance and output indicators for research partnerships. These indicators include conventional measures, such as patents, short-term fluctuations in stock prices, total factor productivity, and R&D expenditure and employment. They also analyzed the following unconventional proxies: technology licensing, citations of patents and scholarly articles, co-authoring between academic and industry scientists, start-up formation, firm retention in a research partnership, the hiring of engineering and science graduates, faculty consulting, firm or research partnership survival, new products developed and commercialized, and sales and employment growth. Many authors have interpreted these indicators as different ways of characterizing the spillover mechanism.

Not surprisingly, management and finance studies have focused mainly on research partnerships involving only firms and have concentrated on explaining short-run financial performance and accounting profitability. Economists, in contrast, have devoted their attention to public–private research partnerships, the search for R&D spillovers, program evaluation, and the effects of consortia, crowding out of private R&D investment, and the impact of research partnerships on total factor productivity.

Many studies of research joint ventures and strategic alliances in the management and finance literatures have relied on the event study methodology, which is based on the capital asset pricing model (CAPM). This method measures the average change in share price that arises when an unanticipated event is announced, which presumably provides new information on the future profitability of companies that experience it. Thus, the use of event studies obviates the need to deal with some of the thorny performance and productivity measurement issues, which were discussed in previous chapters, since event studies focus on stock prices, which reflect market valuations. However, there are numerous problems with this methodology, especially when it comes to the evaluation of SRPs. These issues are discussed in much greater detail in McWilliams and Siegel (1997).

Table 11.1 Recent empirical studies of the effects of research partnerships on economic performance

Author	Type of research partnership	Nature of institutions involved in RP/ unit of observation	Data sets	Methodology	Performance measure
Hagedoorn and Schakenraad (1994)	Strategic technology alliances	Public–private partnership/firm	Maastricht Economic Research Institute on Innovation and Technology (MERIT)–Cooperative Agreements & Technology Indicators (CATI) database	Structural equation modeling (LISREL)	Patents
Sakakibara (1997a)	Japanese research consortia	Public–private partnership/firm	Quantitative and qualitative data on government-sponsored R&D consortia at the project and firm levels	Regression analysis	Qualitative measures of project-related firm R&D expenditure
Sakakibara (1997b)	Japanese research consortia	Public–private partnership/firm	Quantitative and qualitative data on government-sponsored R&D consortia at the project and firm levels	Regression analysis	Contribution of R&D consortia to the establishment of competitive position
Branstetter and Sakakibara (1998)	Japanese research consortia	Public–private partnership/firm	Quantitative and qualitative data on government-sponsored R&D consortia at the project and firm levels	Regression analysis	R&D expenditures, patents
Cockburn and Henderson (1998)	Collaborative relationships involving public and privately financed scientists	Public–private partnership/firm	Co-authorship of scientific papers (from Science Citation Index) involving industry and university scientists in the pharmaceutical industry, authors' calculations of important patents, Compustat	Regression analysis	R&D expenditures, important patents

Zucker et al. (1998)	Relationships involving "star" scientists and US biotechnology firms	Public–private partnership/firm	Authorship of scientific papers reporting genetic-sequence discoveries, data on biotechnology from the North Carolina Biotechnology Center (1992) and Bioscan (1993)	Regression analysis	Birth of biotechnology enterprises
Zucker and Darby (2001)	Relationships involving "star" scientists and Japanese biotechnology firms	Public–private partnership/firm	Data on biotechnology firms from the Biotechnology Guide Japan 1990–1 and the Nikkei Biotechnology Directory	Regression analysis	Patents, number of products developed, number of products on the market
Lerner and Merges (1998)	Strategic technology alliances in the biotechnology industry	Private–private partnership/firm	Database of alliances in the biotechnology industry compiled by Recombinant Capital	Regression analysis	No analysis of performance – authors examine allocation of control rights
Baum et al. (2000)	Strategic technology alliances in the Canadian biotechnology industry	Private–private partnership/firm	Canadian Biotechnology database, which includes information on alliance formation, products, growth, and performance of biotechnology start-ups	Regression analysis	Revenues, R&D employees, R&D expenditure, and patents
Anand and Khanna (2000)	Research joint ventures and licensing contracts	Private–private partnership/firm	Strategic Alliance Database of the Securities Data Company (SDC), CRSP	Event study	Short-term movements in stock prices
Ahuja (2000)	Strategic technology alliances in the chemical industry	Private–private partnership/firm	Dow Jones News Retrieval, Predicast's Funk and Scott (F&S) Index, Chemical Week, Plastics Technology	Regression analysis	Focus of paper is not on performance

(Continued)

Table 11.1 (Continued)

Author	Type of research partnership	Nature of institutions involved in RP/ unit of observation	Data sets	Methodology	Performance measure
Stuart (2000)	Strategic technology alliances in the semiconductor industry	Private–private partnership/firm	Dataquest, Predicast's Funk and Scott (F&S) Index, Lexis-Nexus, Electronic News, Infotrak, Electronic Buyer's News, Electronic Engineering Times, Electronic Business	Regression analysis	Sales growth patents
Chan et al. (1997)	Strategic technology alliances	Private–private partnership/firm	Wall Street Journal Index, Dow Jones News Retrieval, CRSP	Event study	Short-term movements in stock prices
Reuer and Koza (2000)	Research joint ventures	Private–private partnership/firm	Predicast's Funk and Scott (F&S) Index, Lexis-Nexus, and CRSP	Event study	Short-term movements in stock prices
Merchant and Scherdel (2000)	Research joint ventures	Private–private partnership/firm	Dow Jones News Retrieval, CRSP	Event study	Short-term movements in stock prices
Madhavan and Prescott (1995)	Research joint ventures	Private–private partnership/firm	Wall Street Journal Index, Mergers and Acquisitions Magazine, and CSRP	Event study	Short-term movements in stock prices
Koh and Venkatraman (1991)	Research joint ventures	Private–private partnership/firm	Wall Street Journal Index, Mergers and Acquisitions Magazine, and CSRP	Event study	Short-term movements in stock prices
Reuer (2000)	Research joint ventures	Private–private partnership/firm	Predicast's Funk and Scott (F&S) Index, Lexis-Nexus, and CRSP	Event study	Short-term movements in stock prices

Reuer (2001)	Research joint ventures	Private–private partnership/firm	Predicast's Funk and Scott (F&S) Index, Lexis-Nexus, and CRSP	Event study	Short-term movements in stock prices
Link and Bauer (1989)	Research joint ventures	Private–private partnership/firm	Co-operative Research (CORE) Database, authors' survey of R&D intensive firms, Compustat	Regression analysis	Market share, rate of return on company-funded R&D
Vonortas (2000)	Research joint ventures	Private–private partnership/firm	National Co-operative Research Act (NCRA)-RJV database (which also contains data from Compustat and CorpTech)	Descriptive analysis	No analysis of performance – author examines patterns of firm collaboration
Scott (1996)	Environmental research joint ventures	Public–private partnership/firm	Co-operative Research (CORE) database, author's survey of R&D managers	Regression analysis	Self-reported and statistical measures of the effects of cooperation on R&D
Link et al. (1996)	Research joint ventures – SEMATECH	Public–private partnership/firm	Interviews, case studies	Qualitative analysis	Self-reported measures of success
Link (1998)	Government-sponsored R&D projects – ATP (including many RJVs)	Public–private partnership/firm	Interviews, case study	Qualitative analysis	Effects on research productivity
Vonortas (1999)	Government-sponsored R&D projects – ATP (including many RJVs)	Public–private partnership/firm	Interviews, case studies	Qualitative analysis	Effects on research productivity
Link and Scott (1998)	Government-sponsored R&D projects – (including some ATP-supported RJVs)	Public–private partnership/firm	Interviews, case studies	Qualitative analysis	Commercialization results, spillover effects, effects on competitiveness

(Continued)

Table 11.1 (Continued)

Author	Type of research partnership	Nature of institutions involved in RP/ unit of observation	Data sets	Methodology	Performance measure
Irwin and Klenow (1996)	Research joint ventures – SEMATECH	Public–private partnership/firm	Compustat	Regression analysis	Ratio of (private) R&D to sales
Lerner (1999)	Government-funded R&D projects – SBIR	Public–private partnership/firm	GAO surveys of SBIR firms, corporate technology directory, Compustat	Regression analysis	Growth in employment and sales, ability of firms to attract venture capital funding
Griliches and Regev (1998)	Government-funded R&D projects conducted by Israeli manufacturing firms	Public–private partnership/firm	Panel dataset of Israeli manufacturing firms (linking production and R&D data)	Regression analysis	R&D expenditure, total factor productivity
Klette and Moen (1998)	Government-funded R&D projects conducted by Norwegian manufacturing firms	Public–private partnership/firm	Firm-level R&D survey of Norwegian manufacturing firms	Regression analysis	Private R&D expenditure, ratio of (private) R&D to sales
Klette and Moen (1999)	Government-funded R&D projects in information technology conducted by Norwegian manufacturing firms	Public–private partnership/firm	Firm-level R&D survey of Norwegian manufacturing firms	Regression analysis	Private R&D expenditure, ratio of (private) R&D to sales

Wallsten (2000)	Government-funded R&D projects – SBIR	Public–private partnership/firm	Federal Research in Progress (FedRIP) file, SBA's listing of SBIR awardees, Compustat, Dun and Bradstreet	Regression analysis	R&D expenditure
Gompers and Lerner (1999)	Firms financed by venture capital firms (including venture funds sponsored by corporations)	Private–private partnership/firm	Venture Economics, Securities Data Company, VentureOne, Venture Intelligence Database, Million Dollar Directory, Ward's Business directory of US private and public companies, directory of leading private companies. LEXIS/COMPANY/USPRIV, Recombinant Capital, Corporate Technology Directory, CRSP	Regression analysis, event study	Limited analysis of the financial performance of venture capital funds
Hall et al. (2000)	ATP research joint ventures involving universities	Public–private partnership/firm	ATP data, authors' survey of program participants	Regression analysis	No direct measure of performance except termination, qualitative measures of how universities and firms interact
Siegel et al. (1999)	University–industry technology transfer: patents, licenses, start-ups, and sponsored research	Public–private partnership/university	Association of University Technology Managers (AUTM) survey, NSF, and US Census data, interviews	Regression analysis and qualitative research	Total factor productivity of universities
Thursby et al. (2001)	University–industry technology transfer: patents, licenses, start-ups, and sponsored research	Public–private partnership/university	Association of University Technology Managers (AUTM) survey, authors' survey	Regression analysis and qualitative research	Total factor productivity of universities

(Continued)

Table 11.1 (Continued)

Author	Type of research partnership	Nature of institutions involved in RP/ unit of observation	Data sets	Methodology	Performance measure
Mowery et al. (1998)	University–industry technology transfer: patents and licenses	Public–private partnership/ university	Longitudinal data from technology transfer offices at Columbia, Stanford, and the University of California System	Regression analysis	Patents, licensing activity
Mowery and Ziedonis (2000)	University–industry technology transfer: patents and licenses	Public–private partnership/ university	Longitudinal data from technology transfer offices at Columbia, Stanford, and the University of California System	Regression analysis	Patents, licensing activity
Shane and Khurana (1999)	University–industry technology transfer: start-ups	Public–private partnership/firm	Longitudinal data from MIT technology transfer office on all patents, licenses, and start-ups	Regression analysis	Formation of start-ups
Franklin et al. (2001)	University–industry technology transfer: start-ups	Public–private partnership/ university	Authors' qualitative survey of UK technology transfer offices	Correlation analysis and qualitative research	Self-reported measures of success and attitudes towards academic entrepreneurship
Meseri and Maital (2001)	University–industry technology transfer: start-ups	Public–private partnership/ university	Authors' qualitative survey of Israeli technology transfer offices	Regression analysis and qualitative research	Self-reported measures of success

Adams et al. (2001)	University–industry technology transfer: industry–university research centers (IUCRCs), engineering research centers (ERCs), NSF science and technology centers, and industrial laboratories	Public–private partnership/ industrial laboratory	Survey of industrial laboratory technologies, survey of IUCRCs	Regression analysis	Hiring of engineering and science graduates, co-authoring with academics, using faculty members as consultants, patents, R&D expenditure
Gray et al. (2001)	University–industry technology transfer: industry–university research centers (IUCRCs)	Public–private partnership/firm	Survey of IUCRC	Regression analysis	Member retention in IUCRC
Santoro and Gopalakrishnan (2001)	University–industry technology transfer: engineering research centers (ERCs) and industry–university research centers (IUCRCs)	Public–private partnership/firm	Authors' survey of firms who belong to a publicly funded research center	Regression analysis and qualitative research	Self-reported measures of technology transfer activity involving research center
Caloghirou et al. (2001)	University–industry technology transfer–research joint ventures involving universities–European Frameworks Programme	Public–private partnership/firm	STEP to RJV database (consisting of EU-RJV file and RJV-survey (longer questionnaire with numerous qualitative variables))	Regression analysis	Self-reported measures of various aspects of R&D performance (e.g. ability to achieve synergies in research and proxies for absorptive capacity)

(Continued)

Table 11.1 (Continued)

Author	Type of research partnership	Nature of institutions involved in RP/ unit of observation	Data sets	Methodology	Performance measure
Adams et al. (2000)	Cooperative research and development agreements (CRADAs) involving federal laboratories and firms	Public–private partnership/industrial laboratory	Survey of government laboratory R&D, survey of industrial laboratory technologies, Compustat	Regression analysis	Patents, R&D expenditure
Jaffe et al. (1998)	Federal laboratory (Electro-Physics Branch (EPB) of the NASA–Lewis Research Center)	Public–private partnership/firm use of technologies developed at federal laboratory	EPB's patents and citations to those patents by firms	Qualitative analysis	Citations of patents, proxies for absorptive capacity
Siegel et al. (2002)	Science parks (UK)	Public–private partnership/firm	Longitudinal dataset containing information on the characteristics and performance of firms located on and off science parks in the United Kingdom	Regression analysis	Patents, copyrights, new products/services to existing customer base, new products/ services in new markets, total factor productivity of research efforts

Overview of theoretical studies: the impact of research partnerships on economic performance

Three important questions related to economic performance have been addressed and answered in the theoretical literature related broadly to research partnerships and the collaborations that they create. These questions are, following Combs and Link (forthcoming):

- Have research partnerships improved efficiency?
- Have research partnerships increased competition in the marketplace?
- Have research partnerships increased consumer surplus through improved products or faster introduction?

In general, the answer to each question is, yes. A summary of the theoretical literature related to each question is in Table 11.2. We segment the literature in the

Table 11.2 Summary of the policy literature related to the effects of research partnerships on economic performance

Policy question	Finding	Author
Have research partnerships improved efficiency?	Yes – can lower transactions costs	*Transactions cost*: Kogut (1988) Williamson (1996*a*) Williamson (1996*b*) *Strategic management*: Jarillo (1988) Mowery *et al.* (1998) Gomez-Casseres (1996)
	Yes – reduces unnecessary duplicative R&D expenditure via knowledge sharing in endogenous research partnerships	*IO*: Combs (1993) Katz (1986) Kamien *et al.* (1992) Kamien and Zang (1993) *Strategic management*: Pralahad and Hamel (1990)
	Yes – can increase R&D expenditures if significant spillover effects	*IO*: Katz (1986) Motta (1992) D'Aspremont and Jacquemin (1988) DeBondt and Veugelers (1991) DeBondt *et al.* (1992) Kamien *et al.* (1992) Suzumura (1992) Simpson and Vonortas (1994) Vonortas (1994) Brod and Shivakumar (1997)

(Continued)

Table 11.2 (Continued)

Policy question	Finding	Author
	Yes – yields economies of scale, scope, or learning	*IO*: Combs (1993) Petit and Tolwinski (1996) *Strategic management*: Porter (1986) Harrigan (1985) Jarillo (1988) Pralahad and Hamel (1990)
	Yes – reduces risk	*Strategic management*: Harrigan (1985) Kogut (1991) Sanchez (1993) Dixit and Pindyck (1995) Trigeorgis (1996)
Have research partnerships increased competition in the marketplace?	Yes – may decrease concentration	*IO*: Motta (1992) Combs (1993)
	Yes – increases market output and lowers price (via production cost reductions) if significant spillover effects	*IO*: Katz (1986) D'Aspremont and Jacquemin (1988) DeBondt and Veugelers (1991) DeBondt *et al.* (1992) Kamien *et al.* (1992) Suzumura (1992) Simpson and Vonortas (1994) Vonortas (1994) Brod and Shivakumar (1997)
	No – market power	
	Faciliates collusion in product market	*IO*: Martin (1994) Rosenkranz (1995)
	First mover advantage or unique aggregation of resources	*Strategic management*: Porter (1986) Harrigan (1985) Jarillo (1988) Mowery *et al.* (1998) Hamel and Pralahad (1989) Teece (1986)
Have research partnerships increased consumer surplus through improved products or faster introduction?	Yes	*IO*: Poyago-Theotoky (1997)
	But watch out for high pricing due to market power	*Strategic management*: Harrigan (1985) Mowery *et al.* (1998) Pralahad and Hamel (1990) Hamel and Pralahad (1989)

table and below into three economic framework categories – transactions costs, strategic management, and industrial organization.

The transactions costs literature asserts that partnerships, or alliances as they are generally referred, can under certain circumstances offer the most efficient organizational form for R&D. Research partnerships offer advantages not necessarily present in arm's-length contract R&D or in full vertical integration. Two types of transactions efficiencies may arise; if these are strong enough then research partnerships should prevail:

- If there is unified control through an RJV over the R&D activities, then resources of both parties are committed. It is more difficult for one party to take advantage of another that has invested in assets specific to the relationship.
- Tacit knowledge could be more easily transferred.

The strategic management literature suggests that alliances can be used to create and sustain competitive advantage. In particular, alliances may be an efficient way to quickly and uniquely configure resources (clusters of core competencies). Alliances may also give rise to strong relationship capital (strategic networks). The thrust is to increase long-term profitability relative to the industry.

Profitability may increase because of:

- *Cost efficiencies* With alliances, firms do not need to develop all their expertise in house. Conceivably, the duplication of R&D efforts across firms may decline. Or put differently, members of the alliance could specialize in their comparative advantage, yielding economies of scale.

    Synergies between alliance partners could give rise to economies of scope and learning, as well. Economies of scope could occur if the alliance output aids in production of goods across member firms. Economies of learning could stem from transfer of the production experience of one alliance member to another.

The strategic network literature treats the relationships between companies as a specific asset that facilitates R&D transactions within the network. In other words, the network could lower transactions costs. This effect could also represent a social gain.

- *Market power* Well-structured alliances could offer unique products and thereby price above marginal cost. Also, alliances may hasten introduction of a new product. The result may be some degree of monopoly power – either transitory, or sustainable if a first-mover advantage is exploited.

    Aspects of this effect, however, could also benefit consumers. Consumers could value the faster introduction of new products or the improved product features. What results is the well-known trade-off of market power versus increased consumer valuation of differentiated products.

It should be noted that some take a broader view of the above strategy as pro-rather than anti-competitive. That is, the lure of a first-mover advantage or even transitory monopoly power could increase competition to reach the product market.
- *Strategic options*   Alliances could help reduce risk inherent in the uncertainty of expanding into technological development and new markets. Joint ventures give a company an option for acquisition of the venture that could be exercised as information about technology and markets improves over time.

This effect would seem to be a social gain.

Using a game theoretic framework to evaluate equilibrium results, the industrial organization (IO) literature has reached differing conclusions depending on the specific assumptions of the models. According to Vonortas (1997: 77) "It is improbable that the one-fits-all theoretical exercise will be built anytime soon." The models are:

- *Static (non-tournament) models with spillovers*   Predominately, the IO literature on cooperative R&D employs static models that assume spillovers of R&D results from one firm to another. In general, this type of model predicts under-investment in R&D due to the appropriability problem. The literature consistently finds that research alliances tend to alleviate this problem if spillovers are otherwise high. Basically, cooperating firms reduce unnecessary duplicative research and are able to more fully appropriate the results. Whether firms endogenously form such ventures depends on the specific environment.
- *Tournament models with no spillovers*   Surprisingly, few models of cooperative R&D are dynamic in nature, and the small number that are, are difficult to categorize in the table, despite a relatively rich literature on non-cooperative patent races. In the patent race literature, assuming no spillovers, firms tend to over invest in R&D compared to the social optimum and joint profit maximum. Research alliances would therefore be expected to limit this problem, but whether firms form them is questionable; if firms did form research-only joint ventures they would forgo a chance at becoming the sole winner of a patent race. This literature is difficult to categorize in the table for two reasons: one, RJVs do not tend to form endogenously (without government subsidization), and two, reducing research increases efficiency – a counterintuitive result coming about from omitting spillovers from the models.
- *Other dynamic models*   In contrast to the typical tournament models of R&D described above, some dynamic models by, for example, Petit and Tolwinski (1996) and Martin (1994), are easily categorized. Petit and Tolwinski's model shows that learning economies can be accelerated in an RJV. Their model also predicts that an RJV may increase entry to the product market (both dominant and smaller firms enter).

Unfortunately, such an RJV would be unlikely to form without government subsidy. In another dynamic model, Martin discovers that a trigger strategy encouraging product market collusion may evolve in repeated contact between RJV participants.

- *Other models* RJVs may be unlikely to form in the above dynamic models, due to the relatively small benefits from participation compared to the foregone rewards of monopoly profit. Using static models, Combs (1993) and Motta (1992), for example, showed endogenous formation of RJVs despite greater competition in the product market. In the Combs (1993) model, large economies of scale and reduction of unnecessary duplication of research motivate RJV formation. In the Motta (1992) model, vertical product differentiation creates less cut-throat competition in the product market. Differentiation of products lessens the negative impact of a firm's R&D partner becoming its product market competitor. Poyago-Theotoky (1997) also examined vertical differentiation but assumed a research and production joint venture, so her analysis is not categorized in the table, for reasons described below.

Theoretical results on research and production joint ventures are not categorized within the table. Such theory tends to show reduced product market competition but can show more efficiencies.

As a whole, the theoretical literature summarized in Table 11.2 and elaborated upon above makes clear that research partnerships are a socially beneficial organizational form once formed, that is, they positively effect economic performance.

Brief history of research partnerships in the United States

The following brief history of research partnerships in the United States illustrates that the evolution of this research infrastructure institution has combined private–private activities and public–private activities, where public–private activities can take the form of legislative incentives.

One of the first formal research partnerships or collaborations in the United States was the Semiconductor Research Corporation (SRC). In the late 1950s an integrated circuit (IC) industry emerged in the United States. The fledgling industry took form in the 1960s and experienced rapid growth throughout the 1970s. In 1979, when Japanese companies captured 42 percent of the US market for 16 kbit DRAMs (memory devices) and converted Japan's integrated circuit trade balance with the United States from a negative $122 million in 1979 to a positive $40 million in 1980, the US industry became painfully aware that its dominance of the IC industry was being seriously challenged. It was clear to all in the industry that it was in their collective best interest to invest in an organizational structure that would strengthen the industry's position in the global semiconductor marketplace.

The Semiconductor Industry Association (SIA) was formed in 1977 to collect and assemble reliable information about the industry and to develop mechanisms for addressing industry issues with the federal government. In a presentation at an SIA Board Meeting in June 1981, Erich Bloch of IBM described to the industry the nature of the growing competition with Japan and proposed the creation of a semiconductor research cooperative to assure continued US technology leadership. This event witnessed the birth of the SRC. In December 1981 Robert Noyce, then SIA chairman and vice-chairman of Intel, announced the establishment of the SRC was for the purpose of stimulating joint research in advanced semiconductor technology by industry and US universities and to reverse the declining trend in semiconductor research investments. The SRC was formally incorporated in February 1982 with a stated purpose to:

- Provide clearer view of technology needs
- Fund research to address technology needs
- Focus attention on competition
- Reduce research redundancy.

The eleven founding members were Advanced Micro Devices, Control Data Corporation, Digital Equipment Corporation, General Instrument, Honeywell, Hewlett-Packard, IBM, Intel, Monolithic Memories, Motorola, National Semiconductor, and Silicon Systems.

Policy makers soon noticed the virtues of cooperative research in part because such organizational structures had worked well in Japan and in part because the organizational success of the SRC demonstrated that cooperation among competitive firms at the fundamental research level was feasible.

To place the activities surrounding the SRC's formation in a broader perspective, recall that in the early 1980s there was growing concern about the persistent slowdown in productivity growth that first began to plague the US industrial sector in the mid-1970s and about industry's apparent loss of its competitive advantage in world markets, especially firms in the semiconductor industry. The declining US position in the semiconductor industry was well known and in other industries there was widespread concern although the empirical evidence about the competitive position of the United States in international markets was incomplete. However, when the US Department of Commerce (1990) released its 1990 report on emerging technologies, it was apparent to all that the concerns expressed in the early 1980s were quite valid.

As noted in a November 18, 1983 US House of Representatives report about the proposed Research and Development Joint Ventures Act of 1983:

> A number of indicators strongly suggest that the position of world technology leadership once firmly held by the United States is declining. The United States, only a decade ago, with only five percent of the world's population was generating about 75 percent of the world's technology. Now, the U.S. share has declined to about 50 percent and in another ten years, without fundamental changes in our Nation's technological policy... the past trend would suggest that it may be down to only 30 percent. [In hearings], many

distinguished scientific and industry panels had recommended the need for some relaxation of current antitrust laws to encourage the formation of R&D joint ventures.... The encouragement and fostering of joint research and development ventures are needed responses to the problem of declining US productivity and international competitiveness. According to the testimony received during the Committee hearings, this legislation will provide for a significant increase in the efficiency associated with firms doing similar research and development and will also provide for more effective use of scarce technically trained personnel in the United States.

In an April 6, 1984 House report on competing legislation, the Joint Research and Development Act of 1984, the supposed benefits – and recall that at this time it was still too soon for there to be visible benefits coming from the SRC's activities on behalf of the IC industry – of joint R&D were for the first time clearly articulated:

Joint research and development, as our foreign competitors have learned, can be procompetitive. It can reduce duplication, promote the efficient use of scarce technical personnel, and help to achieve desirable economies of scale.... [W]e must ensure to our U.S. industries the same economic opportunities as our competitors, to engage in joint research and development, if we are to compete in the world market and retain jobs in this country.

The National Cooperative Research Act (NCRA) of 1984, after additional revisions in the initiating legislation, was passed on October 11, 1984:

...to promote research and development, encourage innovation, stimulate trade, and make necessary and appropriate modifications in the operation of the antitrust laws.

The NCRA created a registration process, later expanded by the National Cooperative Research and Production Act (NCRPA) of 1993, under which RJVs can disclose their research intentions to the Department of Justice. RJVs gain two significant benefits from such voluntary filings: if subjected to criminal or civil action they are evaluated under a rule of reason that determines whether the venture improves social welfare; and if found to fail a rule-of-reason analysis they are subject to actual rather than treble damages.

One of the more notable RJVs formed and made public through the NCRA disclosure process was SEMATECH (SEmiconductor MAnufacturing TECHnology). It was established in 1987 as a not-for-profit research consortium with an original mission to provide a pilot manufacturing facility where member companies could improve their semiconductor manufacturing process technology. Its establishment came after the Defense Science Board recommended direct government subsidy to the industry in a 1986 report commissioned by the Department of Defense. It was thought that SEMATECH would be the US semiconductor industry's/US government's response to the Japanese government's targeting of their semiconductor industry for global domination. Since its inception, SEMATECH's stated mission has evolved and become more general. The consortium currently defines its mission around solving the technical challenges presented in order to sustain a leadership position for the United States in the global semiconductor industry.

To date, there have been over 800 formal RJVs filed under the NCRA. Certainly, this number is a lower bound on the total number of research partnerships in the United States, even since 1984. Not all are as publicly visible as SEMATECH. Some are quite small, with only two or three members, and others are quite large with hundreds of members. On an average, a joint venture has fourteen members.

As an illustration of the research activity that can successfully occur through a small, less-visible research partnership, consider the Southwest Research Institute Clean Heavy Diesel Engine II joint venture, noticed in the *Federal Register* in early 1996. The eleven member companies, from six countries including the United States, joined together to solve a common set of technical problems. Diesel engine manufacturers were having difficulties, on their own, meeting desired emission control levels. The eleven companies were coordinated by Southwest Research Institute, an independent, non-profit contract research organization in San Antonio, Texas, to collaborate on the reduction of exhaust emissions. The joint research was successful, and each member company took with it fundamental process technology to use in their individual manufacturing facilities to meet desired emission control levels. The joint venture was formally disbanded in mid-1999.

While informal cooperation in research may have been prevalent in the United States for decades, formal RJV relationships are new and it will take longer than a decade and a half to detect, much less dissect, meaningful trends.

Research partnerships remain of policy interest. In the United States, for example, the National Science Foundation (NSF) sponsored a workshop in 2000:

> The purpose of this policy workshop on strategic research partnerships (SRPs) is to evaluate:

- What are the policy needs for indicators related to the formation, activities, and economic consequences of alliances and SRPs? What data and indicators are currently available about alliances and SRPs? What are their strengths and weaknesses?
- How should the Science Resources Studies Division of NSF proceed to develop SRP indicators?

Then, in 2002, NSF co-sponsored with Statistics Canada a second workshop:

> The purpose of the Workshop is to examine the influence of alliances, networks and partnerships on the innovation process. This is done to help

statisticians measure activities associated with these linkages, to inform policy makers, and to promote discussion in the research community.

It is our expectation that research on research partnerships and their broad-based impact on economic performance will dominate the research agendas of scholars for many years to come.

12 Concluding statement

The academic literature that has emerged since the 1987 monograph clearly indicates, as reviewed herein, that scholars have become more microeconomic in their mode of analysis over the past decade-and-one-half. By more microeconomic we mean that they have delved into the black box through the construction of more disaggregated data sets; through the decomposition of R&D by character of use, by source of funding, and most importantly by source of underlying knowledge; and through the decomposition of capital and labor inputs by type and skill. We expect these trends in the field of *technological change* to continue.

As related to the field of *economic performance*, we expect more fundamental advancements. The advancements will likely occur in the broadly defined area of social returns to innovation and technology. Whereas now economic performance is conceptualized narrowly in terms of such indicators as increased profitability or total factor productivity growth, the ensuing decade-and-one-half will likely witness an emphasis on the impact of spillovers of knowledge associated with technological change on society as a whole. As such, economic performance will come to be defined in terms of the social returns that are associated with all investments in knowledge by all of the players – private-sector and public-sector players as well as domestic and international – in the innovation process.

Appendix A
Definition of symbols

Symbol	Definition	Equation first used
Q	Level of output of the economic unit	(2.1)
A	Shift factor that captures the degree of efficiency exhibited in the production process	(2.1)
X	Vector of n inputs $(x_1, \ldots, x_n)$ used in the production process	(2.1)
C	Total cost of production	(2.3)
H	Shift factor, analogous to A, capturing cost efficiency	(2.3)
TFP	Total factor productivity	(2.6)
$\Sigma w_i x_i$	Weighted sum of inputs used in the production process, where w_i refers to the weight of the ith input	(2.7)
$\dfrac{\partial TFP/\partial t}{TFP}$	Percentage rate of growth over time in total factor productivity	(2.8)
A'/A	Technological change or growth in total factor productivity	(2.8)
Π	Firm profitability	(2.9)
P	Shift factor in the profit function	(2.9)
t	Time	(4.1)
K	Capital	(4.1)
L	Labor	(4.1)
f_K	Derivative of the production function with respect to physical capital	(4.2)
f_L	Derivative of the production function with respect to labor	(4.2)
f_{KK}	Second derivative of the production function with respect to physical capital	(4.2)
f_{LL}	Second derivative of the production function with respect to labor	(4.2)
B	Hicksian bias parameter	(4.6)
m	Generalized multi-input and multi-output production function	(4.15)
LQ	Labor quality	(4.19)
h_i	Hours worked by the ith type of labor	(4.19)
v_i	The share of total compensation paid to the ith type of labor	(4.19)

(Continued)

122 Definition of symbols

(Continued)

Symbol	Definition	Equation first used
b_i	Share of total hours worked devoted to the ith labor type	(4.19)
QUALIND	Index of labor quality	(4.20)
m	Total labor hours	(4.20)
α	Elasticity of output with respect to physical capital (also sometimes refers to the share of income devoted to capital)	(4.21)
β	Elasticity of output with respect to labor (also sometimes refers to the share of income devoted to labor)	(4.21)
γ	Parameter reflecting the rate of disembodied technological change	(4.25)
σ	Elasticity of substitution	(4.30)
w	Wage rate	(4.36)
r	Rate of return on capital or the rental price of capital	(4.36)
v	Vintage of capital	(4.37)
$B(v)$	Vintage-specific disembodied shift parameter	(4.37)
$K_v(t)$	Stock of capital from vintage v in operation at period t	(4.37)
$L_v(t)$	Labor used with vintage v capital at period t	(4.37)
$J(t)$	Technology-adjusted capital stock	(4.38)
v_t	Index of technological change	(4.40)
p_K	Rental price of capital	(5.1)
p_L	Wage or price of labor	(5.1)
s_K	Factor share of capital	(5.2)
s_L	Factor share of labor	(5.2)
Q'/Q	Real output growth	(5.3)
K'/K	Real capital growth	(5.3)
L'/L	Real labor growth	(5.3)
p_K'/p_K	Growth in the price of capital	(5.3)
p_L'/p_L	Growth in the price of labor	(5.3)
$F(t)$	Probability a firm adopts an innovation during a specific period of time	(5.10)
$S(t)$	Probability a firm has not adopted an innovation by time t	(5.10)
$h(t)$	Hazard rate, or the conditional probability of adoption	(5.14)
x_{ij}	Output of sector j consumed by sector i	(5.15)
α_{ij}	Input coefficients	(5.15)
$\dfrac{\partial K^T/\partial t}{K^T}$	Growth rate in a translog index of capital	(7.4)
$\dfrac{\partial K/\partial t}{K}$	Directly aggregated index of capital	(7.4)
q_K	Growth rate of factors influencing the effective input of capital services	(7.4)

(Continued)

Definition of symbols

(Continued)

Symbol	Definition	Equation first used
q_L	Growth rate of factors influencing the effective input of labor services	(7.5)
T	Stock of technical capital	(9.1)
OT_i	The ith firm's own or self-financed stock of technical knowledge	(9.2)
PT_i	The ith firm's purchased stock of technical knowledge	(9.2)
GT_i	The ith firm's government-financed stock of technical knowledge	(9.2)
IT	Infrastructure technology that the ith firm utilizes in its production of technology process	(9.2)
RD	Self-financed R&D investment	(9.3)
β	Output elasticity of technical capital	(9.4)
ρ	Marginal product of technical capital	(9.11)
LC	Labor cost function	(10.5)
s_{np}	Relative share of labor costs going to non-production workers	(10.6)
P_{np}	Price or wage of non-production workers	(10.6)
P_p	Price or wage of production workers	(10.6)
R	Stock of R&D capital	(10.7)
C	Stock of computer capital	(10.7)
I	Current flow of investment	(10.7)

Appendix B
Stochastic frontier estimation

To assess relative productivity, many researchers use the stochastic frontier estimation (henceforth, SFE). This method was developed independently by Aigner et al. (1977) and Meeusen and Van den Broeck (1977). SFE generates a production (or cost) frontier with a stochastic error term that consists of two components: a conventional random error ("white noise") and a term that represents deviations from the frontier, or relative inefficiency.

In SFE, a production function, a Cobb–Douglas production function of the following form is estimated:

$$\ln Q_i = \ln \mathbf{X}_i \boldsymbol{\beta} + \varepsilon_i, \tag{A.1}$$

where the subscript i denotes the ith decision-making unit (a plant, firm, industry, or nation), Q represents output, $\mathbf{X}$ is a vector of inputs, $\boldsymbol{\beta}$ is the unknown parameter vector, and ε is an error term with two components, $\varepsilon_i = (V_i - U_i)$ where U_i represents a non-negative error term to account for technical inefficiency, or failure to produce maximal output, given the set of inputs used. V_i is a symmetric error term that accounts for random effects. The standard assumption, following Aigner et al. (1977), is that the U_i and V_i have the following distributions:

$$U_i \sim \text{i.i.d. } N^+(0, \sigma_u^2), \quad U_i \geq 0$$

$$V_i \sim \text{i.i.d. } N(0, \sigma_v^2)$$

That is, the inefficiency term (U_i) is assumed to have a half-normal distribution, that is, a decision-making unit is either on the frontier or below it. An important parameter in this model is $\gamma = \sigma_u^2 / (\sigma_v^2 + \sigma_u^2)$, the ratio of the standard error of technical inefficiency to the standard error of statistical noise, which is bounded between 0 and 1. Note that $\gamma = 0$ under the null hypothesis of an absence of inefficiency, signifying that all of the variance can be attributed to statistical noise.

In recent years, SFE models have been developed that allow the technical inefficiency (relative productivity) term to be expressed as a function of a vector of environmental and organizational variables. For example, Reifschneider and Stevenson (1991) assume that the U_i are independently distributed as truncations at zero of the $N(m_i, \sigma_u^2)$ distribution with:

$$m_i = Z_i \, \delta, \tag{A.2}$$

where **Z** is a vector of environmental, institutional, and organizational variables that are hypothesized to influence efficiency and δ is a parameter vector.

Many researchers use the FRONTIER statistical package, following Coelli (1994), to generate maximum likelihood estimates of the parameter vectors **β** and **δ** from simultaneous estimation of the production function (A.1) and inefficiency term (A.2) equations, using. Based on the estimates values of **β** and **δ**, authors can compute estimates of relative productivity, or what they often term efficiency scores.

Bibliography

Abowd, J., Kramarz, F., and Margolis, D. (1999) "High wage workers and high wage firms," *Econometrica*, 67: 251–333.

Abramovitz, M. (1956) "Resource and output trends in the United States since 1870," *American Economic Review*, 46: 5–23.

Abramovitz, M. (1981) "Welfare quandaries and productivity concerns," *American Economic Review*, 71: 1–17.

Acs, Z. and Audretsch, D.B. (1989) "Patents as a measure of innovative activity," *Kyklos*, 42: 171–80.

Acs, Z. and Audretsch, D.B. (1990) *Innovation and Small Firms*, Cambridge, MA: MIT Press.

Acs, Z., Audretsch, D.B., and Feldman, M.P. (1992) "Real effects of academic research: comment," *American Economic Review*, 82: 363–7.

Acs, Z., Audretsch, D.B., and Feldman, M.P. (1994) "R&D spillovers and recipient firm size," *Review of Economics and Statistics*, 76: 336–40.

Adams, J.D. (1990) "Fundamental stocks of knowledge and productivity growth," *Journal of Political Economy*, 98: 673–702.

Adams, J.D. and Jaffe, A.B. (1996). "Bounding the effects of R&D: an investigation using matched firm and establishment data," *Rand Journal of Economics*, 27: 700–21.

Adams, J.D., Chiang, E.P., and Jensen, J.L. (2000) "The influence of federal laboratory R&D on industrial research," NBER Working Paper No. 7612.

Adams, J.D., Chiang, E.P., and Starkey, K. (2001). "Industry–university cooperative research centers," *Journal of Technology Transfer*, 26 (1–2): 73–86.

Afriat, S.N. (1972) "Efficiency estimation of production functions," *International Economic Review*, 13: 568–98.

Aghion, P. and Howitt, P. (1990) "A model of growth through creative destruction," *Econometrica*, 60: 323–51.

Ahuja, G. (2000). "The duality of collaboration: inducements and opportunities in the formation of interfirm linkages," *Strategic Management Journal*, 21: 317–43.

Aigner, D. and Chu, S. (1968) "On estimating the industry production function," *American Economic Review*, 58: 826–39.

Aigner, D.J., Lovell, C.A.K., and Schmidt, P. (1977) "Formulation and estimation of stochastic frontier production functions," *Journal of Econometrics*, 6: 21–37.

Allen, S.D. and Link, A.N. (1984) "Declining productivity revisited: secular trends or cyclical losses?," *Economics Letters*, 15: 289–93.

Almeida, P. (1996) "Knowledge sourcing by foreign multinationals: patent citation analysis in the U.S. semiconductor industry," *Strategic Management Journal*, 17: 155–65.

Almeida, P. and Kogut, B. (1997) "The exploitation of technological diversity and the geographical localization of innovation," *Small Business Economics*, 9: 21–31.

Almon, C., Jr. (1975) *The American Economy to 1975: An Interindustry Forecast*, New York: Harper & Row.

Anand, B.N. and Khanna, T. (2000). "Do firms learn to create value? The case of alliances," *Strategic Management Journal*, 21: 295–315.

Anderson, S.P., DePalma, A., and Thisse, J.-F. (1992) *Discrete Choice Theory of Product Differentiation*, Cambridge, MA: MIT Press.

Antonelli, C. (1989) "A failure-inducement model of research and development expenditure," *Journal of Economic Behavior and Organization*, 12: 159–80.

Arrow, K.J.M., Chenery, M., Minhas, B. and Solow, R. (1961) "Capital–labor substitution and economic efficiency," *Review of Economics and Statistics*, 43: 225–50.

Association for University Related Research Parks (1998). Worldwide research & science park directory, Washington, DC: Association for University Related Research Parks.

Association of University Technology Managers (AUTM) (1997). The AUTM licensing survey, fiscal year 1996.

Athey, S. and Stern, S. (1998) "An empirical framework for testing theories about complementarity in organizational design," NBER Working Paper No. 6600.

Audretsch, D.B. (1995) *Innovation and Industry Evolution*, Cambridge, MA: MIT Press.

Audretsch, D.B. and Feldman, M.P. (1996) "R&D spillovers and the geography of innovation and production," *American Economic Review*, 86: 630–40.

Audretsch, D.B. and Stephan, P.E. (1996) "Company-scientist locational links: the case of biotechnology," *American Economic Review*, 86: 641–52.

Austin, D.H. (1993) "An event study approach to measuring innovative output: the case of biotechnology," *American Economic Review Papers and Proceedings*, 83: 253–8.

Autor, D.H., Katz, L.F., and Krueger, A.B. (1998) "Computing inequality: have computers changed the labor market?" *Quarterly Journal of Economics*, 113: 1169–215.

Baily, M.N. (1981*a*) "Productivity and the services of capital and labor," *Brookings Papers on Economic Activity*, 1: 1–65.

Baily, M.N. (1981*b*) "The productivity growth slowdown and capital accumulation," *American Economic Review*, 71: 326–31.

Baily, M.N. and Gordon, R.J. (1988) "The productivity slowdown, measurement issues, and the explosion of computer power," *Brookings Papers on Economic Activity: Microeconomics*, 2: 115–200.

Barro, R. and Sala-i-Martin, X. (1998) *Economic Growth*, New York: McGraw Hill.

Bartel, A.P. and Lichtenberg, F.R. (1987) "The comparative advantage of educated workers in implementing new technology," *Review of Economics and Statistics*, 69: 1–11.

Bartel, A.P. and Lichtenberg, F.R. (1990) "The impact of age of technology on employee wages," *Economics of Innovation and New Technology*, 1: 1–17.

Bartel, A.P. and Sicherman, N. (1999). "Technological change and wages: an interindustry analysis," *Journal of Political Economy*, 107: 285–325.

Baudeau, N. (1910) *Premier Introduction à la Philosophie Économique*, edited by A. Dubois, Paris: P. Geuthner [originally 1867].

Baumol, W.J. and Wolff, E.N. (1984) "On interindustry differences in absolute productivity," *Journal of Political Economy*, 92: 1017–34.

Ben-Zion, U. (1984) "The R&D and investment decision and its relationship to the firm's market value: some preliminary results," in Z. Griliches (ed.), *R&D, Patents, and Productivity*, Chicago: University of Chicago Press, 1984.

Ben-Zion, U. and Ruttan, V. (1975) "Money in the production function: an interpretation of empirical results," *Review of Economics and Statistics*, 57: 246–7.

Bercovitz, J., Feldman, M., Feller, I., and Burton, R. (2001) "Organizational structure as determinants of academic patent and licensing behavior: an exploratory study of Duke, Johns Hopkins, and Pennsylvania State Universities," *Journal of Technology Transfer*, 26: 21–35.

Bergson, A. (1983) "Technological progress," in A. Bergson and H.S. Levine (eds), *The Soviet Economy: Toward the Year 2000*, London: George Allen & Unwin.

Berman, E., Bound, J., and Griliches, Z. (1994) "Changes in the demand for skilled labor within U.S. manufacturing industries: evidence from the annual survey of manufacturing," *Quarterly Journal of Economics*, 109: 367–97.

Berman, E., Machin, S. and Bound, J. (1998) "Implications of skill biased technical change: international evidence," *Quarterly Journal of Economics*, 112: 1245–79.

Berndt, E.R. (1980) "Energy price increases and the productivity slowdown in the United States," in *The Decline in Productivity Growth*, Boston: Federal Reserve Bank of Boston.

Berndt, E.R. (1984) "Comment on Jorgenson," in J.W. Kendrick (ed.), *International Comparisons of Productivity and Causes of the Slowdown*, Cambridge, MA: Ballinger Publisher.

Berndt, E.R. and Morrison, C.J. (1995) "High-tech capital formation and economic performance in U.S. manufacturing industries," *Journal of Econometrics*, 65: 9–43.

Berndt, E.R., Griliches, Z., and Rosett, J. (1993) "Auditing the producer price index: micro evidence from prescription pharmaceutical preparations," *Journal of Business and Economic Statistics*, 11: 251–64.

Berndt, E.R., Morrison, C.J., and Rosenblum, L.S. (1992) "High tech capital formation and labor composition in U.S. manufacturing industries: an exploratory analysis," NBER Working Paper No. 4010, March 1992.

Berry, S.T. (1994) "Estimating discrete-choice models of product differentiation," *Rand Journal of Economics*, 25: 242–62.

Betts, J.R. (1997) "The skill bias of technological change in Canadian manufacturing industries," *Review of Economics and Statistics*, 79: 146–50.

Bharadwaj, A.S., Bharadwaj, S.G., and Konsynski, B.R. (1999) "Information technology effects on firm performance as measured by Tobin's q," *Management Science*, 45: 1008–24.

Binswanger, H.P. (1974) "The measurement of technical change biases with many factors of production," *American Economic Review*, 64: 964–76.

Binswanger, H.P. and Ruttan, V.W. (1978) *Induced Innovation: Technology, Institutions and Development*, Baltimore: Johns Hopkins University Press.
Bioscan (1993) Phoenix, AZ: Oryx Press.
Blank, D.M. and Stigler, G.J. (1957) *The Demand and Supply of Scientific Personnel*, New York: National Bureau of Economic Research.
Bound, J., Cummins, C., Griliches, Z., Hall, B., and Jaffe, A. (1984) "Who does R&D and who patents?," in Z. Griliches (ed.) *R&D, Patents, and Productivity*, Chicago: University of Chicago Press.
Bound, J. and Johnson, G. (1992) "Changes in the structure of wages during the 1980's: an evaluation of alternative explanations," *American Economic Review*, 82: 371–92.
Bound, J. and Johnson, G. (1995) "What are the causes of rising wage inequality in the United States?" *Federal Reserve Bank of New York Economic Policy Review*, January 1995, pp. 9–17.
Bozeman, B. and Link, A.N. (1983) *Investments in Technology: Corporate Strategies and Public Policy Alternatives*, New York: Praeger Publishers.
Branstetter, L. and Sakakibara, M. (1998). "Japanese research consortia: a microeconometric analysis of industrial policy," *Journal of Industrial Economics*, 46: 207–35.
Bresnahan, T.F., Brynjolfsson, E. and Hitt, L.M. (2001) "Information technology, workplace organization, and the demand for skilled labor: firm level evidence," NBER Working Paper No. 7136.
Brod, A. and Shivakumar, R. (1997) "R&D cooperation and the joint exploitation of R&D," *Canadian Journal of Economics*, 30: 673–84.
Brynjolfsson, E., Malone, T., Gurbaxani, V., and Kambil, A. (1994) "Does information technology lead to smaller firms," *Management Science*, 40: 1628–44.
Brynjolfsson, E. and Hitt, L.M. (1996) "Paradox lost: firm level evidence on returns to information systems spending," *Management Science*, 42: 541–58.
Bush, V. (1945) *Science – the Endless Frontier*, Washington, DC: US Government Printing Office.
Caballero, R.J. and Jaffe, A.B. (1993) "How high are the giants" shoulders: an empirical assessment of knowledge spillovers and creative destruction in a model of economic growth," in O.J. Blanchard and S. Fischer (eds) *NBER Macroeconomic Annual 1993*, Cambridge, MA: MIT Press.
Cain, L.P. and Patterson, D.G. (1981) "Factor biases and technical change in manufacturing: the American system, 1850–1919," *Journal of Economic History*, 41: 341–60.
Caloghirou, Y., Tsakanikas, A., and Vonortas, N.S. (2001) "University–industry cooperation in the context of the European framework programmes," *Journal of Technology Transfer*, 26: 153–61.
Cantillon, R. (1931) *Essai Sur la Nature du Commerce en Général*, edited and translated by H. Higgs, London: Macmillan.
Carter, A.P. (1970) *Structural Change in the American Economy*, Cambridge, MA: Harvard University Press.
Chan, S.J., Kensinger, A., Keown, A., and Martin, J. (1997) "Do strategic alliances create value?," *Journal of Financial Economics*, 46: 199–222.
Charles River Associates (1981) *Productivity Impacts of Government R&D Labs: The National Bureau of Standards' Semiconductor Technology Program – A Production Function Approach*, Washington, DC: National Bureau of Standards.

Chennells, L. and Van Reenen, J. (1995) "Wages and technology in British plants: do workers get a fair share of the plunder?," mimeographed.
Chinloy, P. (1980) "Sources of quality change in labor input," *American Economic Review*, 70: 108–19.
Christensen, L.R., Cummings, D., and Jorgenson, D.W. (1980) "Economic growth, 1947–73: an international comparison," in J.W. Kendrick and B.N. Vaccara (eds), *New Developments in Productivity Measurement and Analysis*, Chicago: University of Chicago Press.
Christensen, L.R., Jorgenson, D.W., and Lau, L.J. (1971) "Conjugate duality and the trans-cendental logarithmic production function," *Econometrica*, 39: 255–6.
Christensen, L.R., Jorgenson, D.W., and Lau, L.J. (1973) "Transcendental logarithmic production frontiers," *Review of Economics and Statistics*, 55: 28–45.
Christiansen, G.B. and Haveman, R.H. (1980) "The determinants of the decline in measured productivity growth: an evaluation," in *Special Study on Economic Change*, Washington, DC: Congress of the United States.
Christiansen, G.B. and Haveman, R.H. (1981) "Public regulations and the slowdown in productivity growth," *American Economic Review*, 71: 320–5.
Chun, H. (2003) "Information technology and the demand for educated workers: disentangling the impacts of adoption versus use," *Review of Economics and Statistics*, in press.
Clark, K.B. and Griliches, Z. (1984) "Productivity growth and R&D at the business level: results from the PIMS data base," in Z. Griliches (ed.), *R&D, Patents, and Productivity*, Chicago: University of Chicago Press.
Clark, P.K. (1981) "Inflation and productivity growth," paper presented at the Third Annual Conference on Current Issues in Productivity, Rutgers University.
Clark, P.K. (1982) "Inflation and productivity decline," *American Economic Review*, 72: 149–54.
Coase, R.H. (1937) "The nature of the firm," *Economica*, IV: 386–405.
Cockburn, I. and Griliches, Z. (1988) "Industry effects and appropriability measures in the stock market's valuation of R&D and patents," *American Economic Review Papers and Proceedings*, 78: 419–23.
Cockburn, I. and Henderson, R. (1998) "Absorptive capacity, coauthoring behavior, and the organization of research in drug discovery," *Journal of Industrial Economics*, 46: 157–82.
Coelli, T. (1994). "A guide to FRONTIER version 4.1: a computer program for frontier production and cost function estimation," mimeo, Department of Econometrics, University of New England, Armidale.
Coen, R.M. and Hickman, B.G. (1980) "Investment and growth in an econometric model of the United States," *American Economic Review*, 70: 214–19.
Cohen, L. (1994) "When can government subsidize research joint ventures? Politics, economics, and limits to technology policy," *American Economic Review Papers and Proceedings*, 84: 151–63.
Combs, K. (1993) "The role of information sharing in cooperative research and development," *International Journal of Industrial Organization*, 11: 535–51.
Combs, K. and Link, A.N. (forthcoming) "Innovation policy in search of an economic foundation: the case of research partnerships in the United States," *Technology Analysis and Strategic Management*.

Connolly, R.A. and Hirschey, M. (1982) "R&D, market structure, and profits: a value-based approach," *Review of Economics and Statistics*, 66: 682–6.
Copeland, M.A. (1937) "Concepts of national income," in *Studies in Income and Wealth*, New York: National Bureau of Economic Research.
Corporate Technology Information Services (1996 and earlier years), *Corporate technology directory*, Woburn, MA: Corporate Technology Information Service.
Council on Competitiveness (1991) *Gaining New Ground: Technology Priorities for American's Future*, Washington, DC: Council on Competitiveness.
Craig, C.E. and Harris, R.C. (1973) "Total productivity measurement at the firm level," *Sloan Management Review*, 14: 13–29.
Crow, M. and Bozeman, B. (1998) *Limited by Design: R&D Laboratories in the U.S. National Innovation System*, New York: Columbia University Press.
Cuneo, P. and Mairesse, J. (1984) "Productivity and R&D at the firm level in French manufacturing," in Z. Griliches (ed.), *R&D, Patents, and Productivity*, Chicago: University of Chicago Press.
Darby, M.R. (1984) "The U.S. productivity slowdown: a case of statistical myopia," *American Economic Review*, 74: 301–22.
D'Aspremont, C. and Jacquemin, A. (1988) "Cooperative and non-cooperative R&D in duopoly with spillovers," *American Economic Review*, 78: 1133–7.
David, P.A. and van de Klundert, T. (1965) "Biased efficiency growth and capital labor substitution in the U.S., 1899–1960," *American Economic Review*, 55: 357–94.
David, P.A., Hall, B.H., and Toole, A.A. (2000) "Is public R&D a complement or a substitute for private R&D: a review of econometric evidence," *Research Policy*, 29: 497–529.
Davis, S.J. and Haltiwanger, J. (1991) "Wage dispersion between and within U.S. manufacturing plants, 1963–1986," *Brookings Papers on Economic Activity: Microeconomics*, 12, 115–200.
Dean, E., Kunze, K., and Rosenblum, L. (1988) "Productivity change and the measurement of heterogeneous labor inputs," mimeograph.
DeBondt, R. and Veugelers, R. (1991) "Strategic investment with spillovers," *European Journal of Political Economy*, 7: 345–66.
DeBondt, R., Slaets, P., and Cassiman, B. (1992) "The degree of spillovers and the number of rivals for maximum effective R&D," *International Journal of Industrial Organization*, 10: 35–54.
DeLong, B. and Summers, L. (1991) "Equipment investment and economic growth," *Quarterly Journal of Economics*, 102: 445–502.
Denison, E.F. (1962) "United States economic growth," *Journal of Business*, 44: 109–21.
Denison, E.F. (1967) *Why Growth Rates Differ: Postwar Experience in Nine Western Countries*, Washington, DC: Brookings Institution.
Denison, E.F. (1972) "Classification of sources of growth," *Review of Income and Wealth*, 18: 1–25.
Denison, E.F. (1974) *Accounting for U.S. Economic Growth, 1929–1969*, Washington, DC: Brookings Institution.
Denison, E.F. (1979) *Accounting for Slower Economic Growth: The United States in the 1970s*, Washington, DC: Brookings Institution.

Denison, E.F. (1984) "Accounting for slower economic growth: an update," in J.W. Kendrick (ed.), *International Comparisons of Productivity and Causes of the Slowdown*, Cambridge, MA: Ballinger Publishers.

Denison, E.F. (1989) *Estimates of Productivity Change by Industry: An Evaluation and Alternative*, Washington, DC: Brookings Institution.

Diamond, P.A. (1965) "Disembodied technical change in a two-sector model," *Review of Economic Studies*, 32: 161–8.

Dickens, W.T. (1982) "The productivity crisis: secular or cyclical?," *Economics Letters*, 9: 37–42.

Diewert, W.E. (1987) "Index numbers," in Eatwell, J., Milgate, M., and Newman, P. (eds), *The New Palgrave Dictionary of Economics (Volume 2)*, New York: Stockton Press.

Diewert, W.E. and Fox, K.J. (1999) "Can measurement error explain the productivity paradox," *Canadian Journal of Economics*, 32: 251–80.

Dinardo, J.E. and Pischke, J.S. (1997) "The returns to computer use revisited: have pencils changed the wage structure too?," *Quarterly Journal of Economics*, 112: 291–303.

Disney, R., Haskel, J., and Heden, Y. (2000) "Restructuring and productivity change in U.K. manufacturing," University of Nottingham, mimeograph.

Dixit, A.K. and Pindyck R.S. (1995) "The options approach to capital investment," *Harvard Business Review*, 73: 105–15.

Dogramaci, A. (1981) "Perspectives on productivity," in A. Dogramaci (ed.), *Productivity Analysis: A Range of Perspectives*, Boston: Martinus Nijhoff.

Domar, E.D. (1947) "Expansion and employment," *American Economic Review*, 37: 343–55.

Domar, E.D. (1961) "On measurement of technological change," *Economic Journal*, 71: 709–29.

Doms, M., Dunne, T., and Troske, K.R. (1997) "Workers, wages, and technology," *Quarterly Journal of Economics*, 112: 253–90.

Dunne, T. (1994) "Plant age and technology usage in U.S. manufacturing industries," *Rand Journal of Economics*, 25: 488–99.

Dunne, T. and Schmitz, J.A. (1995) "Wages, employer size-wage premia and employment structure: Their relationship to advanced technology usage in U.S. manufacturing establishments," *Economica*, 62: 89–107.

Dunne, T., Haltiwanger, J., and Troske, K.R. (1996), "Technology and jobs: secular change and cyclical dynamics," NBER Working Paper No. 5656.

Dunne, T., Foster, L., Haltiwanger, J., and Troske, K.R. (2000) "Wages and productivity dispersion in U.S. manufacturing: the role of computer investment," NBER Working Paper No. 7465.

Eden, L., Levitas, E., and Martinez, R.J. (1997) "The production, transfer and spillover of technology: comparing large and small multinationals as technology producers," *Small Business Economics*, 9: 53–66.

Eilon, S. and Soesan, J. (1976) "Definitions and prevailing approaches," in S. Eilon *et al.* (eds), *Applied Productivity Analysis for Industry*, Oxford: Pergamon Press.

Entorf, H. and Kramarz, F. (1995) "The impact of new technologies on wages and skills: lessons from matching data on employees and on their firms," mimeograph.

Fabricant, S. (1954) *Economic Progress and Economic Change*, New York: National Bureau of Economic Research.
Farrell, M.J. (1957) "The measurement of production efficiency," *Journal of the Royal Statistical Society, Series A*, 120: 253–90.
Fei, J.C.H. and Ranis, G. (1965) "Innovational intensity and factor bias in the theory of growth," *International Economic Review*, 6: 182–98.
Feldman, M.P. (1994) "Knowledge complementarity and innovation," *Small Business Economics*, 6: 363–72.
Feldman, M.P., Link, A.N., and Siegel, D.S. (2002) *The Economics of Science and Technology*, Norwell, MA: Kluwer Academic Publishers.
Ferguson, C.E. (1971) *The Neoclassical Theory of Production and Distribution*, Cambridge: Cambridge University Press.
Filer, R.K. (1980) "The slowdown in productivity growth: a new look at its nature and causes," in S. Maital and N.M. Meltz (eds) *Lagging Productivity Growth: Causes and Remedies*, Cambridge, MA: Ballinger Publisher.
Foster, L., Haltiwanger, J., and Krizan, B.J. (1998) "Aggregate productivity growth: lessons from microeconomic evidence," NBER Working Paper No. 6803.
Franklin, S., Wright, M., and Lockett, A. (2001). "Academic and surrogate entrepreneurs in university spin-out companies," *Journal of Technology Transfer*, 26 (1–2): 127–41.
Fraumeni, B.M. and Jorgenson, D.W. (1980) "The role of capital in U.S. economic growth, 1948–1976," in G.M. von Furstenberg (ed.), *Capital, Efficiency and Growth*, Cambridge, MA: Ballinger Publisher.
Fraumeni, B.M. and Jorgenson, D.W. (1981) "Capital formation and U.S. productivity growth, 1948–1976," in A. Dogramaci (ed.), *Productivity Analysis: A Range of Perspectives*, Boston: Martinus Nihhoff.
Freeman, R.B. and Medoff, J.L. (1979) "The two faces of unionism," *The Public Interest*, 57: 69–93.
Freeman, R.B. and Medoff, J.L. (1982) "The impact of collective bargaining: can the new facts be explained by monopoly unionism?," mimeographed.
Freeman, R.B. and Medoff, J.L. (1984) *What Do Unions Do?* New York: Basic Books.
Gera, S., Gu, W., and Lee, F. (1999) "Information technology and labour productivity growth: an empirical analysis for Canada and the United States," *Canadian Journal of Economics*, 32: 384–407.
Gilbert, R.J. and Newberry, D.M.G. (1982) "Preemptive patenting and the persistence of monopoly," *American Economic Review*, 72: 514–26.
Gilbert, R.J. and Newberry, D.M.G. (1984) "Uncertain innovation and the persistence of monopoly: comment," *American Economic Review*, 74: 238–42.
Geroski, P. (2000) "Models of technology diffusion," *Research Policy*, 29: 603–26.
Glaeser, E., Kallal, H., Scheinkman, J., and Shleifer, A. (1992) "Growth of cities," *Journal of Political Economy*, 100: 1126–52.
Gold, B. (1955) *Foundations of Productivity Analysis*, Pittsburgh: University of Pittsburgh Press.
Gollop, F.M. and Roberts, M.J. (1981) "Imported intermediate input: its impact on sectoral productivity in U.S. manufacturing," in A. Dogramaci and N.E. Adam (eds), *Aggregate and Industry-Level Productivity Analyses*, Boston: Martinus Nijhoff.

134 Bibliography

Gomez-Casseres, B. (1996) *The Alliance Revolution: The New Shape of Business Rivalry*, Cambridge, MA: Harvard University Press.

Gompers, P. and Lerner, J. (1999) *The Venture Capital Cycle*, Cambridge, MA: MIT Press.

Gordon, R.J. (1979) "The end-of-expansion phenomenon in short-run productivity behavior," *Brookings Papers on Economic Activity*, 2: 447–60.

Grabowski, H.G. (1968) "The determinants of industrial research and development: a study of the chemical, drug, and petroleum industries," *Journal of Political Economy*, 76: 156–9.

Gray, D.O., Lindblad, M., and Rudolph, J. (2001) "University-based industrial research consortia: a multivariate analysis of member retention," *Journal of Technology Transfer*, 26: 247–54.

Greenan, N. and Mairesse, J. (1996) "Computers and productivity in France: some evidence," NBER Working Paper No. 5836.

Griliches, Z. (1957) "Hybrid corn: an exploration in the economics of technical change," *Econometrica*, 25: 501–22.

Griliches, Z. (1969) "Capital-skill complementarity," *Review of Economics and Statistics*, 51: 465–8.

Griliches, Z. (1970) "Note on the role of education in production functions and growth accounting," in L. Hansen (ed.), *Education and Income*, New York: Columbia University Press.

Griliches, Z. (1973) "Research in growth accounting," in B.R. Williams (ed.), *Science and Technology in Economic Growth*, New York: John Wiley.

Griliches, Z. (1979) "Issues in assessing the contribution of R&D to productivity growth," *Bell Journal of Economics*, 10: 92–116.

Griliches, Z. (1980*a*) "R&D and the productivity slowdown," *American Economic Review*, 70: 343–8.

Griliches, Z. (1980*b*) "Returns to research and development expenditures in the private sector," in J.W. Kendrick and B.N. Vaccara (eds), *New Developments in Productivity Measurement and Analysis*, Chicago: University of Chicago Press.

Griliches, Z. (1981) "Market value, R&D, and patents," *Economics Letters*, 7: 183–7.

Griliches, Z. (1986) "Productivity growth, R&D, and basic research at the firm level in the 1970s," *American Economic Review*, 76: 141–54.

Griliches, Z. (1996) "Education, human capital, and growth: a personal perspective," NBER Working Paper No. 5426.

Griliches, Z. (1996) "The discovery of the residual: a historical note," *Journal of Economic Literature*, 34: 339–74.

Griliches, Z. (1998) *R&D and Productivity: The Econometric Evidence*, National Bureau of Economic Research for the University of Chicago Press, Chicago: University of Chicago Press.

Griliches, Z. and Lichtenberg, F.R. (1984), "R&D and productivity growth at the industry level: is there still a relationship?," in Z. Griliches (ed.), *R&D, Patents, and Productivity*, Chicago: University of Chicago Press, pp. 465–96.

Griliches, Z. and Mairesse, J. (1984) "Productivity and R&D at the firm level," in Z. Griliches (ed.), *R&D, Patents, and Productivity*, Chicago: University of Chicago Press.

Griliches, Z. and Regev, H. (1998) "An econometric evaluation of high-tech policy in Israel," mimeograph.

Grossman, G. and Helpman, E. (1991a) *Innovation and Growth in the Global Economy*, Cambridge, MA: MIT Press.
Grossman, G. and Helpman, E. (1991b) "Quality ladders in the theory of economic growth," *Review of Economic Studies*, 58: 43–61.
Grossman, J.H., Morgan, R.P., and Reid, R.P. (2001) "Contributions of academic research to industrial performance in five industry sectors," *Journal of Technology Transfer*, 26: 143–52.
Hagedoorn, J., Link, A.N., and Vonortas, N.S. (2000) "Research partnerships," *Research Policy*, 29: 567–86.
Hagedoorn, J. and Schakenraad, J. (1994) "The effect of strategic technology alliances on company performance," *Strategic Management Journal*, 15: 291–309.
Hall, B.H., Griliches, Z., and Hausman, J.A. (1986) "Patents and R&D: is there a lag?," *International Economic Review*, 27: 265–83.
Hall, B.H., Link, A.N., and Scott, J.T. (2000) "Universities as research partners," NBER Working Paper No. 7643.
Hall, B.H., Link, A.N., and Scott J.T. (forthcoming) "Universities as research partners," *Review of Economics and Statistics*, in press.
Hall, B.H. and van Reenan, J. (2000) "How effective are fiscal incentives for R&D? A review of the evidence," *Research Policy*, 29: 449–69.
Hall, R.E. and Jones, C.I. (1996) "The productivity of nations," NBER Working Paper No. 5812.
Hamel, G.P. and Pralahad, C.K. (1989), "Strategic intent," *Harvard Business Review*, 67: 63–76.
Harrigan, K.R. (1985) *Strategy for Joint Ventures*, Lexington, MA: Lexington Books.
Harrod, R.F. (1946) "An essay in dynamic theory," *Economic Journal*, 49: 14–33.
Harrod, R.F. (1948) *Toward a Dynamic Economics*, London: Macmillan.
Haskel, J. (1999) "Small firms, contracting-out, computers and wage inequality: evidence from U.K. manufacturing," *Economica*, 66: 1–21.
Haskel, J. and Heden, Y. (1999) "Computers and the demand for skilled labour: industry and establishment-level panel evidence for the U.K.," *Economic Journal*, 109: 68–79.
Hayes, R.H. and Abernathy, W.J. (1980) "Managing our way to economic decline," *Harvard Business Review*, 58: 67–77.
Hébert, R.F. and Link, A.N. (1988) *The Entrepreneur: Mainstream Views and Radical Critiques*, New York: Praeger Publishers.
Henderson, R., Jaffe, A., and Trajtenberg, M. (1998) "Universities as a source of commercial technology: a detailed analysis of university patenting, 1965–1988," *Review of Economics and Statistics*, 80: 119–27.
Henrici, S.B. (1981) "How deadly is the productivity disease?," *Harvard Business Review*, 59: 123–9.
Hicks, J.R. (1932) *Theory of Wages*, London: Macmillan.
Higgins, R.S. and Link, A.N. (1981) "Federal support of technological growth in industry: some evidence of crowding-out," *IEEE Transactions on Engineering Management*, EM-28: 86–88.
Hirsch, B.T. and Addison, J.T. (1986) *The Economic Analysis of Unions: New Approaches and Evidence*, London: George Allen & Unwin.
Hirsch, B.T. and Link, A.N. (1984) "Unions, productivity, and productivity growth," *Journal of Labor Research*, 5: 29–37.

Hitt, L.M. and Brynjolfsson, E. (1996) "Productivity, business profitability, and consumer surplus: three different measures of information technology value," *MIS Quarterly*, 21: 121–42.

Holemans, B. and Sleuwagen, L. (1988) "Innovation expenditures and the role of government in Belgium," *Research Policy*, 17: 375–9.

Hudson, E.A. and Jorgenson, D.W. (1978*a*) "Energy policy and U.S. economic growth," *American Economic Review*, 68: 118–23.

Hudson, E.A. and Jorgenson, D.W. (1978*b*) "Energy prices and the U.S. economy, 1972–1976," *Natural Resources Journal*, 18: 887–97.

Hulten, C.R. (2000) "Total factor productivity: a short biography," NBER Working Paper No. 7471.

Irwin, D. and Klenow, P. (1996) "High-tech R&D subsidies-estimating the effects of SEMATECH," *Journal of International Economics*, 40: 323–44.

Jaffe, A. (1989) "Real effects of academic research," *American Economic Review*, 79: 957–70.

Jaffe, A.B., Fogarty, M.S., and Banks, B.A. (1998) "Evidence from patents and patent citations on the impact of NASA and other federal labs on commercial innovation," *Journal of Industrial Economics*, 46: 183–206.

Jaffe, A.B., Trajtenberg, M., and Henderson, R. (1993) "Geographic localization of know-ledge spillovers as evidenced by patent citations," *Quarterly Journal of Economics*, 108: 577–98.

Jarillo, J. (1988) "On strategic networks," *Strategic Management Journal*, 19: 31–41.

Johansen, L. (1959) "Substitution versus fixed production coefficients in the theory of economic growth: a synthesis," *Econometrica*, 27: 157–76.

Jones, C.I. (1995). "R&D-based models of economic growth," *Journal of Political Economy*, 103: 759–84.

Jorgenson, D.W. (1984) "The role of energy in productivity growth," in J.W. Kendrick (ed.), *International Comparisons of Productivity and Causes of the Slowdown*, Cambridge, MA: Ballinger Publishers.

Jorgenson, D.W. (1996) "Technology in growth theory," in J.C. Fuhrer and J.S. Little (eds), *Technology and Growth*, Boston: Federal Reserve Bank of Boston.

Jorgenson, D.W. and Griliches, Z. (1967) "The explanation of productivity change," *Review of Economics and Statistics*, 34: 249–84.

Jorgenson, D.W., Gollop, F.W., and Fraumeni, B. (1987) *Productivity and U.S. Economic growth, 1979–1985*, Cambridge: Harvard University Press.

Jorgenson, D.W. and Stiroh, K. (1995) "Computers and growth," *Economics of Innovation and New Technology*, 3: 295–316.

Jorgenson, D.W. and Stiroh, K. (2000) "Raising the speed limit: U.S. economic growth in the information age," *Brookings Papers on Economics Activity* 1: 125–211.

Juhn, C., Murphy, K.M., and Pierce, B. (1993) "Wage inequality and the rise in returns to skill," *Journal of Political Economy*, 101: 410–42.

Kalt, K.P. (1978) "Technological change and factor substitution in the United States: 1929–1967," *International Economic Review*, 19: 761–75.

Kamien, M.I., Mueller, E., and Zang, I. (1992) "Research joint ventures and R&D cartels," *American Economic Review*, 82: 1293–306.

Kamien, M.I. and Zang, I. (1993) "Competing research joint ventures," *Journal of Economics and Management Strategy*, 2: 24–40.

Katz, L.F. and Murphy, K. (1992) "Changes in relative wages, 1963–1987: supply and demand factors," *Quarterly Journal of Economics*, 107: 35–78.
Katz, M.L. (1986) "An analysis of cooperative research and development," *Rand Journal of Economics*, 17: 527–43.
Kelley, M.R. (1994) "Productivity and information technology," *Management Science*, 1994, 40: 1406–25.
Kendrick, J.W. (1956) "Productivity trends: capital and labor," *Review of Economics and Statistics*, 38: 248–57.
Kendrick, J.W. (1973) *Postwar Productivity Trends in the United States, 1948–1969*, Princeton: National Bureau of Economic Research.
Kendrick, J.W. (1980) "Remedies for the productivity slowdown in the United States," in S. Maital and N.M. Meltz (eds), *Lagging Productivity Growth: Causes and Remedies*, Cambridge, MA: Ballinger Publisher.
Kendrick, J.W. (1982) "International comparisons of recent productivity trends," in W. Fellner (ed.) *Essays in Contemporary Economic Problems: Demand, Productivity, and Population*, Washington, DC: American Enterprise Institute.
Kendrick, J.W. and Grossman, E.S. (1980) *Productivity in the United States: Trends and Cycles*, Baltimore: Johns Hopkins University Press.
Klein, B.H. (1979) "The slowdown in productivity advances: a dynamic explanation," in C.T. Hill and J.M. Utterback (eds), *Technological Innovation for a Dynamic Economy*, New York: Pergamon Press.
Klette, T.J. and Griliches, Z. (1997) "Empirical patterns of firm growth and R&D investment: a quality ladder model interpretation," NBER Working Paper No. 5945.
Klette, T.J. and Moen, J. (1998). "R&D investment responses to R&D subsidies: a theoretical analysis and a microeconometric study," mimeograph.
Klette, T.J. and Moen, J. (1999) "From growth theory to technology policy-coordination problems in theory and practice," *Nordic Journal of Political Economy*, 25: 53–74.
Kogut, B. (1991) "Joint ventures and the option to expand and acquire," *Management Science*, 37: 19–33.
Kogut, B. (1998) "Joint venture: theoretical and empirical perspectives," *Strategic Management Journal*, 9: 319–32.
Koh, J. and Venkatraman, N. (1991) "Joint venture formation and stock market reactions: an assessment in the information technology sector," *Academy of Management Journal*, 34: 869–92.
Krueger, A.B. (1993) "How computers have changed the wage structure: evidence from microdata," *Quarterly Journal of Economics*, 108: 33–61.
Kuznets, S. (1962) "Inventive activity: problems of definition and measurement," in R. Nelson (ed.), *The Rate and Direction of Inventive Activity*, Princeton: National Bureau of Economic Research.
Lanjouw, J.O., Pakes, A., and Putnam, J. (1998) "How to count patents and value intellectual property: the use of patent renewal and application data," *Journal of Industrial Economics*, 46: 405–42.
Lau, L. and Tokutsu, I. (1992) "The impact of computer technology on the aggregate productivity of the United States: an indirect approach," mimeograph.
Lehr, W. and Lichtenberg, F.R. (1998) "Computer use and productivity growth in U.S. federal government agencies, 1987 to 1992," *Journal of Industrial Economics*, 46: 257–79.

Lehr, W. and Lichtenberg, F.R. (1999) "Information and its impact on productivity: firm-level evidence from government and private data sources, 1977–1993," *Canadian Journal of Economics*, 32: 335–62.

Leontief, W.W. (1953) *Studies in the Structure of the American Economy*, New York: Oxford University Press.

Lerner, J. (1999) "The government as venture capitalist: the long-run impact of the SBIR Program," *Journal of Business*, 72: 285–318.

Lerner, J. and Merges, R.P. (1998) "The control of technology alliances: an empirical analysis of the biotechnology industry," *Journal of Industrial Economics*, 46: 125–56.

Levy, F. and Murnane, R.J. (1997) *The New Basic Skills*, Cambridge, MA: MIT Press.

Leyden, D.P. and Link, A.N. (1991) "Why are government and private R&D complements?," *Applied Economics*, 23: 1673–81.

Leyden, D.P. and Link, A.N. (1992) *Government's Role in Innovation*, Norwell, MA: Kluwer Academic Publishers.

Leyden, D.P. and Link, A.N. (1993) "Tax policies affecting R&D: an international comparison," *Technovation*, 13: 17–25.

Leyden, D.P. and Link, A.N. (1999) "Federal laboratories and research partners," *International Journal of Industrial Organization*, 17: 572–92.

Leyden, D.P., Link, A.N., and Bozeman, B. (1989) "The effects of governmental financing on firms' R&D activities: a theoretical and empirical investigation," *Technovation*, 9: 561–75.

Licht, G. and Moch, D. (1999) "Innovation and information technology in services," *Canadian Journal of Economics*, 32: 363–83.

Lichtenberg, F.R. (1984) "The relationship between federal contract R&D and company R&D," *American Economic Review*, 74: 73–78.

Lichtenberg, F.R. (1987) "The effect of government funding on private industrial research and development: a re-assessment," *Journal of Industrial Economics*, 36: 97–104.

Lichtenberg, F.R. (1988) "The private R&D investment response to federal design and technical competitions," *American Economic Review*, 78: 550–9.

Lichtenberg, F.R. (1992) "R&D investments and international productivity differences," NBER Working Paper No. 4161.

Lichtenberg, F.R. (1995) "The output contributions of computer equipment and personnel: a firm-level analysis," *Economics of Innovation and New Technology*, 3: 201–17.

Lichtenberg, F.R. and Griliches, Z. (1989) "Errors of measurement in output deflators," *Journal of Business and Economic Statistics*, 7: 1–9.

Lichtenberg, F.R. and Siegel, D. (1987) "Productivity and changes in ownership of manufacturing plants," *Brookings Papers on Economic Activity*, 3: 643–73.

Lichtenberg, F.R. and Siegel, D. (1990) "The effect of leveraged buyouts on productivity and related aspects of firm behavior," *Journal of Financial Economics*, 27: 165–94.

Lichtenberg, F.R and Siegel, D. (1991) "The impact of R&D investment on productivity – new evidence using linked R&D–LRD data," *Economic Inquiry*, 29: 203–28.

Lindbeck, A. (1983) "The recent slowdown of productivity growth," *Economic Journal*, 93: 13–34.

Link, A.N. (1981) "Basic research and productivity increase in manufacturing: some additional evidence," *American Economic Review*, 71: 1111–12.
Link, A.N. (1982*a*) "A disaggregated analysis of industrial R&D: product versus process innovation," in D. Sahal (ed.), *The Transfer and Utilization of Technical Knowledge*, Lexington, MA: D.C. Health.
Link, A.N. (1982*b*) "The impact of federal research and development spending on productivity," *IEEE Transactions on Engineering Management*, EM-29: 166–9.
Link, A.N. (1982*c*) "Productivity growth, environmental regulations and the composition of R&D," *Bell Journal of Economics*, 13: 548–54.
Link, A.N. (1983) "Interfirm technology flows and productivity growth," *Economics Letters*, 11: 179–84.
Link, A.N. (1987) *Technological Change and Productivity Growth*, Char: Harwood Academic Publishers.
Link, A.N. (1996*a*) *Evaluating Public Sector Research and Development*, New York: Praeger Publishers.
Link, A.N. (1996*b*) "On the classification of industrial R&D," *Research Policy*, 25: 397–401.
Link, A.N. and Bauer, L.L. (1989) *Cooperative Research in U.S. Manufacturing: Assessing Policy Initiatives and Corporate Strategies*, Lexington, MA: D.C. Heath.
Link, A.N. and Kapur, P. (1994) "A note on the diffusion of flexible manufacturing systems technology," *Economics Letters*, 46: 369–74.
Link, A.N., Paton, D., and Siegel, D.S. (2002) "An analysis of policy initiatives to promote strategic research partnerships," *Research Policy*, 31: 1459–66.
Link, A.N. and Rees, J. (1990) "Firm size, university based research and the returns to R&D," *Small Business Economics*, 2: 25–32.
Link, A.N. and Scott, J.T. (1998) *Public Accountability: Evaluating Technology-Based Institutions*, Norwell, Mass.: Kluwer Academic Publishers.
Link, A.N. and Scott, J.T. (2002*a*) "Explaining observed licensing agreements: toward a broader understanding of technology flows," 11: 211–31.
Link, A.N. and Scott J.T. (2002*b*) "The growth of Research Triangle Park," *Small Business Economics*, in press.
Link, A.N. and Siegel, D.S. (2002) "Unions and technology adoption: a qualitative analysis of the use of real-time control systems in U.S. coal firms," *Journal of Labor Research*, 23: 615–30.
Link, A.N. and Tassey, G. (1993) "The technology infrastructure of firms: investments in infratechnology," *IEEE Transactions on Engineering Management*, 40: 312–15.
Link, A.N. and Zmud, R.W. (1987) "Alternative sources of technical knowledge," *Economics Letters*, 15: 91–103.
Lucas, R.E., Jr. (1988) "On the mechanics of economic development," *Journal of Monetary Economics*, 22: 3–42.
Lynch, L.M. and Osterman, P. (1989) "Technological innovation and employment in telecommunications," *Industrial Relations*, 28: 188–205.
Machin, S. (1996) "Changes in the relative demand for skills in the UK labour market," in A. Booth and D. Snower (eds), *Acquiring Skills*, Cambridge: Cambridge University Press.
Machlup, F. (1980) *Knowledge and Knowledge Production*, Princeton: Princeton University Press.

140 Bibliography

McCallum, B.T. (1996) "Neoclassical vs. endogenous growth analysis: an overview," NBER Working Paper No. 5844.

McGuckin, R.H. and Nguyen, S.V. (1995) "On productivity and plant ownership change: evidence from the longitudinal research database," *Rand Journal of Economics*, 26: 257–76.

McGuckin, R.H. and Stiroh, K.J. (1999) "Computers and productivity: are aggregation effects important?," *Economic Inquiry*, 32: 114–28.

McGuckin, R.H., Streitwieser, M.L., and Doms, M. (1998) "The effect of technology use on productivity growth," *Economics of Innovation and New Technology*, 7: 1–27.

McWilliams, A. and Siegel, D. (1997) "Event studies in management research: theoretical and empirical issues," *Academy of Management Journal*, 40: 626–57.

McWilliams, A., Siegel, D., and Teoh, S.H. (1999). "Issues in the use of the event study methodology: a critical analysis of corporate social responsibility studies," *Organizational Research Methods*, 2: 340–65.

Maddison, A. (1984) "Comparative analysis of the productivity situation in the advanced capitalist countries," in J.W. Kendrick (ed.), *International Comparisons of Productivity and Causes of the Slowdown*, Cambridge, MA: Ballinger Publishers.

Madhavan, R. and Prescott, J.E. (1995) "Market value of joint ventures: the effects of industry information-processing load," *Academy of Management Journal*, 38: 900–15.

Mankiw, G., Romer, D., and Weil, D.N. (1992) "A contribution to the empirics of economic growth," *Quarterly Journal of Economics*, 107: 407–37.

Mansfield, E. (1961) "Technical change and the rate of imitation," *Econometrica*, 29: 741–66.

Mansfield, E. (1963) "The speed of response of firms to new technologies," *Quarterly Journal of Economics*, 77: 290–311.

Mansfield, E. (1968) *Industrial Research and Technological Change*, New York: W.W. Norton.

Mansfield, E. (1980) "Basic research and productivity increase in manufacturing," *American Economic Review*, 70: 863–73.

Martin, S. (1994) "R&D joint ventures and tacit product market collusion," *European Journal of Political Economy*, 11: 733–41.

Martin, S. and Scott, J.T. (2000) "The nature of innovation market failure and the design of public support for private innovation," *Research Policy*, 29: 437–48.

Meeusen, W. and Van den Broeck, J. (1977) "Efficiency estimation from Cobb-Douglas production functions with composed errors," *International Economic Review*, 18: 435–44.

Merchant, H. and Scherdel, D. (2000) "How do international joint ventures create shareholder value?" *Strategic Management Journal*, 21: 723–37.

Meseri, O. and Maital, S. (2001) "A survey analysis of university technology transfer in Israel: evaluation of projects and determinants of success," *Journal of Technology Transfer*, 26: 115–25.

Milgrom, P. and Roberts, J. (1990) "The economics of modern manufacturing," *American Economic Review*, 80: 511–28.

Mills, F.C. (1952) *Productivity and Economic Progress*, National Bureau of Economic Research Occasional Paper 38.

Minasian, J.R. (1962) "The economics of research and development," in R.R. Nelson (ed.), *The Rate and Direction of Inventive Activity: Economic and Social Factors*, New York: National Bureau of Economic Research.

Mincer, J. (1989) "Human capital responses to technological change in the labor market," NBER Working Paper No. 3581.

Mishel, L. (1988) *Manufacturing Numbers: How Inaccurate Statistics Conceal US Industrial Decline*, Washington, DC: Economy Policy Institute.

Mishel, L. and Bernstein, J. (1994) "Is the technology black box empty?," mimeograph.

Moroney, J. (1972) *The Structure of Production in American Manufacturing*, Chapel Hill, NC: University of North Carolina Press.

Morrison, C.J. (1997) "Assessing the productivity of information technology equipment in U.S. manufacturing industries," *Review of Economics and Statistics*, 79: 471–81.

Morrison, C.J. and Siegel, D.S. (1997) "External capital factors and increasing returns in U.S. manufacturing," *Review of Economics and Statistics*, 79: 647–54.

Morrison Paul, C.J. and Siegel, D.S. (1999) "Scale economies and industry agglomeration externalities: a dynamic cost function approach," *American Economic Review*, 89: 272–90.

Morrison Paul, C.J. and Siegel, D.S. (2001) "The impacts of technology, trade, and outsourcing on employment and labor composition," *Scandinavian Journal of Economics*, 103: 241–64.

Motta, M. (1992) "Cooperative R&D and vertical product differentiation," *International Journal of Industrial Organization*, 10: 643–61.

Mowery, D.C. and Ziedonis, A.A. (2000) "Numbers, quality and entry: how has the Bayh–Dole Act affected U.S. university patenting and licensing?" in A. Jaffe, J. Lerner, and S. Stern (eds), *Innovation Policy and the Economy*, Cambridge, MA: MIT Press.

Mowery, D.C., Oxley, J.E., and Silverman, B.S. (1998) "Technological overlap and interfirm cooperation for the resource-based view of the firm," *Research Policy*, 27: 507–23.

Mowery, D.C., Nelson, R.R., Sampat, B., Ziedonis, A.A. (1999) "The effects of the Bayh–Dole act on U.S. university research and technology transfer: an analysis of data from Columbia University, the University of California, and Stanford University," *Research Policy*, 29: 729–40.

Mueller, D.C. (1967) "The firm decision process: an econometric investigation," *Journal of Political Economy*, 75: 58–87.

Murphy, K.M. and Welch, F. (1989) "Wage premiums for college graduates: recent growth and possible explanations," *Educational Researcher*, 22: 18–24.

Murphy, K.M. and Welch, F. (1992) "The structure of wages," *Quarterly Journal of Economics*, 107: 215–26.

Myers, S. and Marquis, D.G. (1969) *Successful Industrial Innovations*, Washington, DC: National Science Foundation.

Nadiri, M.I. (1970) "Some approaches to the theory and measurement of total factor productivity: a survey," *Journal of Economic Literature*, 8: 1137–77.

Nadiri, M.I. (1980) "Sectoral productivity slowdown," *American Economic Review*, 70: 349–52.

Nadiri, M.I. and Mohnen, P. (1981) "Sources of the productivity slowdown: an international comparison," mimeographed.

Bibliography

Nadiri, M.I. and Schankerman, M.A. (1981) "Technical change, returns to scale, and the productivity slowdown," *American Economic Review*, 71: 314–19.

Nelson, R.R. (1964) "Aggregate production functions and medium-range growth projections," *American Economic Review*, 54: 575–606.

Nelson, R.R. (1965) "The CES production function and economic growth projections," *Review of Economics and Statistics*, 47: 326–8.

Nelson, R.R. (1981) "Research on productivity growth and productivity differences: dead ends and new departures," *Journal of Economic Literature*, 19: 1029–64.

Nelson, R.R. (1993) *National Innovation Systems: A Comparative Analysis*, Oxford: Oxford University Press.

Nelson, R.R. (1997) "How new is new growth theory?," *Challenge*, 40: 29–58.

Nelson, R.R. (2001) "Observations on the post-Bayh–Dole rise of patenting at American universities," *Journal of Technology Transfer*, 26 (1–2): 13–19.

Nelson, R.R. and Phelps, E.S. (1966) "Investment in Human Technological Diffusion and Economic Growth," *American Economic Review*, 56: 69–75.

Nelson, R.R. and Winter, S.G. (1982) *An Evolutionary Theory of Economic Change*, Cambridge, MA: Harvard University Press.

Nerlove, M. (1967) "Recent empirical studies of the CES and related production functions," in M. Brown (ed.), *The Theory and Empirical Analysis of Production*, New York: Columbia University Press.

Nishimizu, M. and Page, J.M., Jr. (1982) "Total factor productivity growth, technological progress and technical efficiency change: dimensions of productivity change in Yugoslavia, 1965–78," *Economic Journal*, 92: 920–36.

Nordhaus, W.D. (1980) "Policy responses to the productivity slowdown," in *The Decline in Productivity Growth*, Boston: Federal Reserve Bank of Boston.

Norsworthy, J.R., Harper, M.J., and Kunze, K. (1979) "The slowdown in productivity growth: an analysis of some contributing factors," *Brookings Papers on Economic Activity*, 3: 387–421.

North Carolina Biotechnology Center (1992) *North Carolina Biotechnology Center U.S. Companies Database*, Research Triangle Park, NC: North Carolina Biotechnology Center.

Oliner, S.D. and Sichel, D. (1994) "Computers and output growth revisited: how big is the puzzle," *Brookings Papers on Economic Activity*, 2: 273–315.

Organization for Economic Co-operation and Development (OECD) (2001a) *Economic Outlook, No. 68*, Paris, Organization for Economic Co-operation and Development.

Organization for Economic Co-operation and Development (OECD) (2001b) *OECD Productivity Manual: A Guide to the Measurement of Industry-Level and Aggregate Productivity Growth*, Paris: OECD.

Pakes, A. (1985) "On Patents, R&D, and the stock market rate of return," *Journal of Political Economy*, 93: 390–409.

Pakes, A. and Griliches, Z. (1980) "Patents and R&D at the firm level: a first report," *Economics Letters*, 5: 377–81.

Pakes, A. and Griliches, Z. (1984) "Patents and R&D at the firm level: a first look," in Z. Griliches (ed.), *R&D, Patents, and Productivity*, Chicago: University of Chicago Press.

Park, K.S. (1996) "Economic growth and multiskilled workers in manufacturing," *Journal of Labor Economics*, 12: 254–85.

Park, S.H. and Kim, D. (1997) "Market valuation of joint ventures: characteristics and wealth gains," *Journal of Business Venturing*, 12: 83–108.
Parsons, D.J., Gottlieb, C.C., and Denny, M. (1993) "Productivity and computers in Canadian banking," *Journal of Productivity Analysis*, 4: 91–110.
Perloff, J.M. and Wachter, M.L. (1980) "The productivity slowdown: a labor problem?," in *The Decline in Productivity Growth*, Boston: Federal Reserve Bank of Boston.
Petit, M.L. and Tolwinski, B. (1996) "Technology sharing cartels and industrial structure," *International Journal of Industrial Organization*, 15: 77–101.
Petit, P. and Soete, L. (eds) (2001) *Technology and the Future of European Employment*, Cheltenham, UK: Edward Elgar.
Porter, M.E. (1986) "Changing patterns of international competition," *California Management Review*, XXVII: 9–40.
Poyago-Theotoky, J. (1997) "Research joint ventures and product innovation: some welfare aspects," *Economics of Innovation and New Technology*, 5: 51–73.
Poyago-Theotoky, J., Beath, L. and Siegel, D.S. (2002) "Universities and fundamental research: reflections on the growth of university–industry partnerships," *Oxford Review of Economic Policy*, 18: 10–21.
Pralahad, C.K. and Hamel, G. (1990) "The core competence of the corporation," *Harvard Business Review*, 68: 79–91.
Prevezer, M. (1997) "The dynamics of industrial clustering in biotechnology," *Small Business Economics*, 9: 255–71.
Quesnay, F. (1888) *Oeuvres Economiques et Philosophiques*, edited by A. Oncken, Frankfurt: M.J. Baer.
Raa, T. and Wolff, E.N. (2001) "Outsourcing of services and the productivity recovery in U.S. manufacturing in the 1980s and 1990s," *Journal of Productivity Analysis*, 16: 149–65.
Rasche, R.M. and Tatom, J.A. (1977a) "The effects of the new energy regime on economic capacity, production, and prices," *Federal Reserve Bank of St. Louis Review*, 59: 2–12.
Rasche, R.M. and Tatom, J.A. (1977b) "Energy resources and potential GNP," *Federal Reserve Bank of St. Louis Review*, 59: 10–21.
Rees, A. (1980) "On interpreting productivity change," in S. Maital and N.M. Meltz (eds), *Lagging Productivity Growth: Causes and Remedies*, Cambridge, MA: Ballinger Publishers.
Regev, H. (1998) "Innovation, skilled labor, technology and performance in Israeli industrial firms," *Economics of Innovation and New Technology*, 5: 301–24.
Reifschneider, D. and Stevenson, R. (1991) "Systematic departures from the frontier: a framework for the analysis of firm inefficiency," *International Economic Review*, 32: 715–23.
Reilly, K.T. (1995) "Human capital and information," *Journal of Human Resources*, 30: 1–18.
Reinganum, J. (1985) "Innovation and industry evolution," *Quarterly Journal of Economics*, 100: 81–98.
Reuer, J.J. (2000) "Parent firm performance across international joint venture lifecycle stages," *Journal of International Business Studies*, 31: 1–20.
Reuer, J.J. (2001) "From hybrids to hierarchies: shareholder wealth effects of joint venture buyouts," *Strategic Management Journal*, 22: 27–44.

Reuer, J.J. and Koza, M.P. (2000) "Asymmetric information and joint venture performance: theory and evidence for domestic and international joint ventures," *Strategic Management Journal*, 21: 81–88.

Romeo, A. (1975) "Inter-industry and inter-firm differences in the rate of diffusion of an innovation," *Review of Economics and Statistics*, 57: 311–19.

Romeo, A. (1977) "The rate of imitation of a capital embodied process innovation," *Economica*, 44: 63–69.

Romer, P.M. (1986) "Increasing returns and long run growth," *Journal of Political Economy*, 94: 1002–37.

Romer, P.M. (1990) "Endogenous technological change," *Journal of Political Economy*, 98: S71–S102.

Rosenkranz, S. (1995) "Innovation and cooperation under vertical product differentiation," *International Journal of Industrial Organization*, 13: 1–22.

Sahal, D. (1981) *Patterns of Technological Innovation*, Reading, MA: Addison-Wesley.

Sahal, D. (1985) "Foundations of technometrics," *Technological Forecasting and Social Change*, 27: 1–37.

Sakakibara, M. (1997*a*) "Heterogeneity of firm capabilities and co-operative research and development: an empirical examination," *Strategic Management Journal*, 18: 143–64.

Sakakibara, M. (1997*b*) "Evaluating government sponsored R&D consortia in Japan: who benefits and how?," *Research Policy*, 26: 447–73.

Salter, W.E.G. (1966) *Productivity and Technical Change*, Cambridge: Cambridge University Press.

Sanchez, R.A. (1993) "Strategic flexibility, firm organization, and managerial work in dynamic markets: a strategic-options perspective," in P. Shrivastava, A. Huff, and J.E. Dutton (eds), *Advances in Strategic Management*, Greenwich, CT: JAI Press.

Santoro, M. and Gopalakrishnan, S. (2001) "Relationship dynamics between university research centers and industrial firms: their impact on technology transfer activities," *Journal of Technology Transfer*, 26: 163–71.

Sato, R. (1980) "The impact of technical change on the holotheticity of production functions," *Review of Economic Studies*, 47: 767–76.

Saxenian, A. (1990) "Regional networks and the resurgence of Silicon Valley," *California Management Review*, 32: 89–111.

Schankerman, M.A. (1981), "The effects of double-counting and expensing on the measured returns to R&D," *Review of Economics and Statistics*, 63: 454–8.

Schankerman, M.A. (1998) "How valuable is patent protection? Estimates by technology field," *Rand Journal of Economics*, 29: 77–107.

Scherer, F.M. (1965*a*) "Firm size, market structure, opportunity and the output of patented inventions," *American Economic Review*, 55: 1097–125.

Scherer, F.M. (1965*b*) "Invention and innovation in the Watt–Boulton steam-engine venture", *Technology and Culture*, 6: 165–87.

Scherer, F.M. (1982) "Inter-industry technology flows and productivity growth," *Review of Economics and Statistics*, 6: 627–34.

Scherer, F.M. (1983*a*) "The propensity to patent," *International Journal of Industrial Organization*, 1: 107–28.

Scherer, F.M. (1983*b*) "R&D and declining productivity growth," *American Economic Review*, 73: 215–18.

Schmookler, J. (1952) "The changing efficiency of the American economy, 1869–1938," *Review of Economics and Statistics*, 34: 214–31.
Schmookler, J. (1966) *Invention and Economic Growth*, Cambridge, MA: Harvard University Press.
Schultz, T.W. (1953) *The Economic Organization of Agriculture*, New York: McGraw-Hill.
Schultz, T.W. (1980) "Investments in entrepreneurial ability," *Scandinavian Journal of Economics*, 82: 437–48.
Schumpeter, J.A. (1934) *Theory of Economic Development*, Cambridge, MA: Harvard University Press.
Schumpeter, J.A. (1950) *Capitalism, Socialism and Democracy*, New York: Harper & Row.
Schumpeter, J.A. (1928) "The instability of capitalism," *Economic Journal*, 38: 361–86.
Schumpeter, J.A. (1939) *Business Cycles*, New York: McGraw-Hill.
Schwalbach, J. and Zimmermann, K.F. (1991) "A poisson model of patenting and firm structure in Germany," in Z. Acs and D.B. Audretsch (eds), *Innovation and Technological Change: An International Comparison*, Ann Arbor: University of Michigan Press.
Shane, S. and Khurana, R. (1999) "Career experiences and firm foundings," mimeograph.
Shleifer, A. (2000) *Inefficient markets*, New York: Oxford University Press.
Sichel, D. (1997) *The Computer Revolution: An Economic Perspective*, Washington, DC: Brookings Institution.
Siegel, D.S. (1994). "Errors in output deflators revisited: unit values and the PPI," *Economic Inquiry*, 32: 11–32.
Siegel, D.S. (1995) "Errors of measurement and the recent acceleration in manufacturing productivity growth," *Journal of Productivity Analysis*, 6: 297–320.
Siegel, D.S. (1997) "The impact of computers on manufacturing productivity growth: a multiple-indicators, multiple-causes approach," *Review of Economics and Statistics*, 79: 68–78.
Siegel, D.S. (1999) *Skill-Biased Technological Change: Evidence from a Firm-Level Survey*, Kalamazoo, MI: W.E. Upjohn Institute Press.
Siegel, D. and Griliches, Z. (1992) "Purchased services, outsourcing, computers, and productivity in manufacturing," in Z. Griliches (ed.), *Output Measurement in the Service Sector*, Chicago: University of Chicago Press.
Siegel, D.S., Waldman, D., and Link, A.N. (1999) "Assessing the impact of organizational practices on the productivity of university technology transfer offices: an exploratory study," NBER Working Paper No. 7256.
Siegel, D.S., Westhead, P., and Wright, M. (2002) "Assessing the impact of science parks on the research productivity of firms: evidence from the U.K," mimeograph.
Siegel, D.S., Thursby, J.G., Thursby, M.C., and Ziedonis, A.A. (2001) "Organizational issues in university–industry technology transfer: an overview of the symposium issue," *Journal of Technology Transfer*, 26: 5–11.
Siegel, R. (1979) "Why has productivity slowed down?," *Data Resources U.S. Review*, 1: 59–65.
Simpson, R.D. and Vorortas, N.S. (1994) "Cournot equilibrium with imperfectly appropriable R&D," *Journal of Industrial Economics*, XLII: 79–92.

146 Bibliography

Sinai, A. and Stokes, H.H. (1972) "Real money balances: an omitted variable from the production function," *Review of Economics and Statistics*, 54: 290–6.

Smith, A. (1937) *An Inquiry into the Nature and Causes of the Wealth of Nations*, New York: Random House [originally 1776].

Solow, R.M. (1956) "A contribution to the theory of economic growth," *Quarterly Journal of Economics*, 70: 65–94.

Solow, R.M. (1957) "Technical change and the aggregate production function," *Review of Economics and Statistics*, 39: 312–20.

Solow, R.M. (1960) "Investment in technical progress," in K.J. Arrow *et al.* (eds), *Mathematical Methods in the Social Sciences, 1959*, Stanford: Stanford University Press.

Solow, R.M. (1962) "Technical progress, capital formation and economic growth," *American Economic Review*, 52: 76–86.

Solow, R.M. (1967) "Some recent developments in the theory of production," in M. Brown (ed.), *The Theory and Empirical Analysis of Production*, Princeton: National Bureau of Economic Research.

Stigler, G.J. (1947) *Trends in Output and Employment*, New York: National Bureau of Economic Research.

Stiroh, K.J. (1998) "Computers, productivity, and input substitution," *Economic Inquiry*, 36: 175–91.

Stiroh, K.J. (2001) "What drives productivity growth," *FRBNY Economic Policy Review*, 16: 37–59.

Stolarick, K.M. (1999) "IT spending and firm productivity: additional evidence from the manufacturing sector," mimeograph.

Stoneman, P. (1983) *The Economic Analysis of Technological Change*, Oxford: Oxford University Press.

Stuart, T.E. (2000) "Interorganizational alliances and the performance of firms: a study of growth and innovation rates in a high-technology industry," *Strategic Management Journal*, 21: 791–812.

Sudit, E.F. and Finger, N. (1981) "Methodological issues in aggregate productivity analysis," in A. Dogramaci and N.R. Adam (eds), *Aggregate and Industry-Level Productivity Analyses*, Boston: Martinus-Nijhoff.

Summers, R. and Heston, A. (1988) "A new set of international comparisons of real product and price level estimates for 130 countries, 1950–1985," *Review of Income and Wealth*, 34: 1–25.

Suzumura, K. (1992) "Cooperative and non-cooperative R&D in oligopoly with spillovers," *American Economic Review*, 82: 1307–20.

Swan, T.W. (1956) "Economic growth and capital accumulation," *Economic Record*, 32: 334–61.

Tassey, G. (1982) "Infratechnolgies and the role of government," *Technological Forecasting and Social Change*, 21: 163–80.

Tassey, G. (1992) *Technology Infrastructure and Competitive Position*, Norwell, MA: Kluwer Academic Publishers.

Teece, D.J. (1986) "Profiting from technological innovation: implications for integration, collaboration, licensing and public policy," *Research Policy*, 15: 285–305.

Terleckyj, N.E. (1974) *Effects of R&D on the Productivity Growth of Industries: An Exploratory Study*, Washington, DC: National Planning Association.

Terleckyj, N.E. (1982) "R&D and the U.S. industrial productivity in the 1970s," in D. Sahal (ed.), *The Transfer and Utilization of Technical Knowledge*, Lexington, MA: D.C. Health.
Tether, B.S. (2002) "Who co-operates for innovation, and why: an empirical analysis," *Research Policy*, 31: 947–67.
Thursby, J.G., Jensen, R., and Thursby, M.C. (2001) "Objectives, characteristics and outcomes of university licensing: a survey of major U.S. universities," *Journal of Technology Transfer*, 26: 59–72.
Tinbergen, J. (1942) "Zur theorie der langfirstigen wirtschaftsentwicklung," *Weltwirtschaftliches Archiv*, 1: 511–49.
Trajtenberg, M. (1990). *Economic Analysis of Product Innovation: The Case of CT Scanners*, Cambridge, MA: Harvard University Press
Trigeorgis, L. (1996) *Real Options – Managerial Flexibility and Strategy in Resource Allocation*, Cambridge: MIT Press.
Triplett, J. (1988) "Price index research and its influence of data: a historical review," mimeograph.
Troske, K. (1994) "Evidence on the employer size-wage premium from worker-establishment matched data," US Census Bureau Center for Economic Studies Working Paper 94-10.
US Department of Commerce, Technology Administration (1990) *Emerging Technologies: A Survey of Technical and Economic Opportunities*, Washington, DC: US Department of Commerce.
Usher, A.P. (1954) *A History of Mechanical Inventions*, Cambridge, MA: Harvard University Press.
Van Reenen, J. (1996) "The creation and capture of rents: wages and innovation in a panel of U.K. companies," *Quarterly Journal of Economics*, 111: 195–226.
Van Reenen, J. (1997) "Employment and technological innovation: evidence from U.K. manufacturing firms," *Journal of Labor Economics*, 15: 255–84.
Verdoorn, P.J. (1980) "Verdoorn's law in retrospect: a comment," *Economic Journal*, 90: 382–5.
Vonortas, N.S. (1994) "Interfirm cooperation with imperfectly appropriable research," *International Journal of Industrial Organization*, 12: 413–35.
Vonortas, N.S. (1997) *Cooperation in Research and Development*, Boston: Kluwer Academic Publishers.
Vonortas, N.S. (1999). "Business diversification through research joint ventures: the advanced technology program," Final report to the Advanced Technology Program, NIST, Gaithersburg, MD.
Vonortas, N.S. (2000) "Multimarket contact and inter-firm cooperation in R&D," *Journal of Evolutionary Economics*, 10: 243–71.
Wallsten, S. (2000). "The effects of government–industry R&D programs on private R&D: the case of the small business innovation research program," *Rand Journal of Economics*, 31: 82–100.
Walters, A.A. (1963) "A note on economies of scale," *Review of Economics and Statistics*, 45: 425–6.
Welch, F. (1970) "Education in production," *Journal of Political Economy*, 78: 35–59.
Williamson, O.E. (1996a) "Economics and organization: a primer," *California Management Review*, 38: 131–46.

Williamson, O.E. (1996b) *The Mechanics of Governance*, Oxford: Oxford University Press.

Zucker, L.G. and Darby, M.R. (2001) "Capturing technological opportunity via Japan's star scientists: evidence from Japanese firms' biotech patents and products," *Journal of Technology Transfer*, 26: 37–58.

Zucker, L.G., Darby, M.R., and Brewer, M.B. (1998) "Intellectual human capital and the birth of U.S. biotechnology enterprises," *American Economic Review*, 88: 290–306.

Index

Abernathy, W.J. 58
Abramovitz, M. 14, 56
accounting profitability 11, 101
Acs, Z. 37–8, 68–9
Adams, J.D. 69, 109–10
Addison, J.T. 57
advanced materials 76
Advanced Micro Devices 116
Afriat, S.N. 24
Aghion, P. 17
Ahuja, G. 103
Aigner, D. 24
Aigner, D.J. 124
aircraft industries 65
Allen, S.D. 51
Almeida, P. 69
Almon, C., Jr. 41
Anand, B.N. 103
Anderson, S.P. 18
Annual Survey of Manufacturers (ASM) 90
antitrust laws 100
Antonelli, C. 76
Arrow, K.J.M. 29
Association of University Technology Managers (AUTM) 101
Athey, S. 96
Audretsch, D.B. 37–8, 68–9
Austin, D. 38
Autor, D.H. 84, 89

Baily, M.N. 53–5
Barro, R. 18
Bartel, A.P. 80, 83, 87–8
Baudeau, Abbé N. 2
Bauer, L.L. 77–8, 105
Baum, J. 103
Baumol, W.J. 26
Bayh–Dole Act of 1980 59
Belgium 42–3

Ben-Zion, V. 38
Bergson, A. 43
Berman, E. 80–1, 83, 86, 88
Berndt, E.R. 50, 55, 87–8, 92, 95
Bernstein, J. 86, 88
Berry, S.T. 18
Betts, J.R. 84, 88
Bharadwaj, A.S. 93
Binswanger, H.P. 29
biotechnology 76
Blank, D.M. 76
Bound, J. 37–8, 79, 81
Bozeman, B. 61, 65
Branstetter, L. 102
Bresnahan, T.F. 82, 97
Brod, A. 111–12
Brynjolfsson, E. 92, 94–5
Bush, V. 66; linear model 66

Caballero, R.J. 18
Cain, L.P. 29
Caloghirou, Y. 109
Canada 33, 43–4, 51; banks 92; manufacturing industries 88; workers 89
Cantillon, R. 2
capital: equipment 16, 61, 79; formation 51; investments 51; productivity index 25; rate of productivity growth in 42; stock, depreciation of 54
capital asset pricing model (CAPM) 101
capital-saving technological change 21
capital-skill complementarity 81
Carter, A.P. 40
Census of Manufacturers (CM) 90
Chan, S.J. 104
Charles River Associates 70
Chennells, L. 85, 90–1
Chinloy, P. 26
Christensen, L.R. 32–3, 44

150   *Index*

Christiansen, G.B. 25, 56
Chu, S. 24
Clark, P.K. 54
Coase, R.H. 61
Cobb–Douglas production function 27–8, 31, 96
Cockburn, I. 38, 102
Coelli, T. 125
Coen, R.M. 55
Combs, K. 111–12, 115
competition, perfect 15
competitive strategy 60
computers: capital 36; effects of 91; empirical studies of impact on economic performance 91–6; hardware and software 96
constant elasticity of substitution (CES) production function 29–30
Control Data Corporation 116
cooperative research and development agreements (CRADAs) 98
Copeland, M.A. 9
cost efficiencies 113
Council on Competitiveness 76
Craig, C.E. 27
creative destruction 17
cross function 8
Crow, M. 65
Cuneo, P. 73
Current Population Survey 90
cyclical shocks 50–1

Darby, M.R. 50
D'Aspremont, C. 111–12
David, P.A. 30, 76
Davis, S.J. 89
Dean, E. 26
DeBondt, R. 111–12
1990 Decennial Census, demographic data 90
decision-making, decentralized 97
Defense Science Board 117
deflated-price approach 26
DeLong, B. 18
demographic changes in inputs 51
Denison, E.F. 34, 46, 56, 73
developed countries 42
development 67
Diamond, P.A. 22
Dickens, W.T. 51
Diewert, W.E. 50
Digital Equipment Corporation 116
digital-imaging technology 76
Dinardo, J.E. 84, 91
Disney, R. 25

Dixit, A.K. 112
Dogramaci, A. 40
Domar, E.D. 15, 28
Doms, M. 84
DRAMs (memory devices) 115
Dunne, T. 68, 82, 85, 89–90, 93

economic efficiency 1
economic good, diffusion of 68
economic growth: early theoretical and empirical studies of 13; sources of 2
economic performance 10–12, 120
economics literature 9, 38
economy, steady-state growth rate 16
Eden, L. 69
efficiency wage models 88
Eilon, S. 41
employee–employer data sets, matched 90
employment share of scientists and engineers 88
energy prices 55
energy-shock hypothesis 55
Engineering Research Centres (ERCs), National Science Foundation-sponsored 98
engineering and science graduates, hiring of 101
Entorf, H. 86, 91
entrepreneurial process, integrated model of 62–4
entrepreneurship 57–8
environmental compliance 56
environmental and work safety program regulations 56
evolutionary model of growth 24

Fabricant, S. 14
factor markets 15
factor-saving classification schemes 20–3
Farrell, M.J. 41
federal laboratories 63
Federal Register 118
federally funded research and development centers (FFRDCs) 98
Fei, J.C.H. 22
Feldman, M.P. 69, 74
Ferguson, C.E. 22
Filer, R.K. 55
Finger, N. 24
firm-level surveys of production 101
firms: market acceptance of innovation of 11; market value of patents of 11; production process 79; R&D spending 62; technology strategy 61; with university research relationships 78

Foster, L. 25
France 33, 42–4, 51–2, 65, 89–90
Franklin, S. 108
Fraumeni, B.M. 33, 52
Freeman, R.B. 57
French Physiocrats 2
FRONTIER statistical package 125

General Instrument 116
Gera, S. 93
Germany 33, 51, 64–5
Geroski, P. 38
Gilbert, R.J. 18
Glaeser, E. 69
global competitiveness 1; of American firms 58
Gold, B. 41
Gollop, F.M. 33
Gomez-Casseres, B. 111
Gompers, P. 107
Gompertz diffusion model 39
goods bias, new 50
Gopalakrishnan, S. 109
Gordon, R.J. 27, 51
government regulation 56
Grabowski, H.G. 68
Gray, D.O. 109
The Great Depression 46
Greenan, N. 94
Griliches, Z. 15, 17–18, 34–5, 38–9, 46–7, 68, 70, 72–3, 75–6, 79–81, 92, 95, 106
Gross Domestic Product (GDP), share of capital in 16
Grossman, E.S. 34–5, 46–7, 57
Grossman, G. 17–18
Grossman, J.H. 99
growth: accounting 34–6; annual rates in productivity measures 43
growth theory: literature 2; new 14, 16–19; old 14–16, 18

Hagedoorn, J. 100, 102
Hall, B.H. 37–8, 68–9, 74–5, 107
Hall, R.E. 18
Haltiwanger, J. 89
Hamel, G.P. 111–12
Harrigan, K.R. 112
Harris, R.C. 27
Harrod, R.F. 15, 22–3, 28–9, 80; classification scheme 22
Haskel, J. 83
Haveman, R.H. 25, 56
Hayes, R.H. 58
Hébert, R.F. 2, 17

Heden, Y. 83
Helpman, E. 17–18
Henderson, R. 38, 102
Henrici, S.B. 49
Heston, A. 19
Hewlett-Packard 116
Hickman, B.G. 55
Hicks, J.R. 21–4, 28–9, 80; technological change 21
Higgins, R.S. 76
Hildreth, A. 84
Hirsch, B.T. 57
Hirschey, M. 38
Hitt, L.M. 92, 94–5
Holemans, B. 76
Honeywell 116
Howitt, P. 17
Hudson, E.A. 55
human capital 12, 18; role of 17

IBM 116
ignorance, measure of 14
industrial organization (IO) literature 114
industry-level data from foreign countries 88
industry–university cooperative research centres (IUCRCs) 98
industry wage bill 88
inflation and energy prices 54–5
information technology (IT): effects on workers and economic performance 79; impact on economic growth 36; investment in 96; use of 97
infrastructure technology 63, 78
innovation 1–2, 7–8, 64; counts 91; economic value of 63; and firm size relationship 68; as a source for technological change 15; stimulus 61
innovative firms 90
input: growth, underestimation of 47; markets 15; prices, errors in measuring 48
input–output decision framework 40
intangible tools 5
integrated circuit (IC) industry 115
Intel 116
intellectual property laws 100
international comparisons of Real National Accounts 19
invention 7–8
investment: in computers 88, 92; in R&D 70
Irwin, D. 106
Israel 89
Italy 33, 43–4, 51, 64

Jacquemin, A. 111–12
Jaffe, A.B. 18, 38, 69, 110
Japan 33, 43–4, 51–2, 56, 64, 76; companies 115; growth rates in 42
Jarillo, J. 111–12
Johansen, L. 31
Johnson, G. 79
Jones, C.I. 18
Jorgenson, D.W. 16, 26, 33–4, 35–6, 52, 55, 80, 95–6
Juhn, C. 89

Kalt, K.P. 30
Kapur, P. 39
Katz, L.F. 89
Kendrick, J.W. 13, 30, 34–5, 43, 46–7, 51, 56–7; discrete arithmetic index of productivity change 30
Khanna, T. 103
Khurana, R. 108
Kicht, G. 93
Klein, B.H. 57
Klenow, P. 106
Klette, T.J. 17–18, 106
knowledge: advances in 34; alternative sources of 49; base of technology 6; investment costs 16; production-function model of 68; as a source of innovation 15; spillovers, studies of 69
Kogut, B. 69, 111–12
Koh, J. 104
Korea 33; manufacturing industries, multi-skilled workers in 88
Koza, M.P. 104
Kramarz, F. 86, 91
Krueger, A.B. 87, 89
Kuznets, S. 7, 15

labor: blue collar 88; division of 1; economists 88; markets 89; productivity 10, 12, 25–7, 42, 51; skilled 80; unskilled 80
labor-augmenting technical change 89
labor-saving: improvement 27; technological change 21
Lanjouw, J.O. 37
latent variables model 88
Lau, L. 95
Lehr, W. 93–4
Leontief, W.W. 40; productivity measures 40
Lerner, J. 103, 106–7
Levy, F. 89
Leyden, D.P. 18, 74, 76, 78

licensing and sponsored research agreements 98
Lichtenberg, F.R. 18, 25, 47, 59, 73, 75–6, 80, 87–8, 92–5
Lindbeck, A. 55
Longitudinal Research Database (LRD) 90
Loveman, G. 95
Lucas, R.E., Jr. 17
lunar landings 65
Lynch, L.M. 87, 89

Maastricht Economic Research Institute on Innovation and Technology – Cooperative Agreements and Technology Indicators file (MERIT-CATI) 100
McCallum, B.T. 15
McGuckin, R.H. 25, 93–4
Machin, S. 85, 91
Machlup, F. 6; notion of perception 6
McWilliams, A. 101
Maddison, A. 51–2, 54
Madhavan, R. 104
Mairesse, J. 73, 94
Maital, S. 108
management: decision framework 40; and finance studies 101
managerial talent 54
Mankiw, G. 18, 25
Mansfield, E. 38–9, 68, 75–6
market: environment 60; power 113; stock price effects, long-run 11; valuation of assets 55
Marquis, D.G. 38
Martin, S. 99, 112–14
Medoff, J.L. 57
Meeusen, W. 124
Merchant, H. 104
Merges, R.P. 103
Meseri, O. 108
Milgrom, P. 96
Mills, F.C. 13
Minasian, J.R. 72
Mincer, J. 89
Mishel, L. 46, 86, 88
Moch, D. 93
Moen, J. 106
Mohnen, P. 44, 51
Monolithic Memories 116
Moroney, J. 29
Morrison, C.J. 69, 81, 92, 94–6
Morrison Paul, C.J. 82, 91
Motorola 116
Motta, M. 111–12, 115

Mowery, D.C. 108, 111
Mueller, D.C. 68
multi-indicators multiple causes model 47
Murnane, R.J. 89
Murphy, K. 89
Myers, S. 38

Nadiri, M.I. 21, 25, 44, 51, 73
National Academy of Engineering (NAE) 99
National Bureau of Economic Research 15
National Cooperative Research Act (NCRA) 58, 77–8, 117
National Cooperative Research Act (NCRA)–Research Joint Venture (NCRA–RJV) database 100
National Cooperative Research and Production Act (NCRPA) 117
National Income and Product Accounts 14
National Institutes of Health 65
National Longitudinal Survey (NLS) 90
National Science Foundation (NSF) 65–7, 118; Cooperative Research (CORE) database 100; R&D classification scheme 66; Science Resources Studies Division 118; *see also* Engineering Research Centers
National Semiconductor 116
Nelson, R.R. 13, 16, 24, 30, 32, 79
Nelson and Winter, evolutionary model 25
neoclassical growth model 16
neoclassical tradition 25
Nerlove, M. 29
Netherlands, the 33, 44, 52
neutral technological change 21
Newberry, D.M.J. 18
newness, characteristics of 7
New York City 15
Nguyen, S.V. 25
Nishimizu, M. 24
nonfarm business economy 50
non-production workers 88
Nordhaus, W.D. 50
Norsworthy, J.R. 46, 52–5

office equipment, high-technology 88
Oliner, S.D. 36, 92, 95–6
optimization 63
Organisation for Economic Cooperation and Development (OECD) 45, 66; countries 3, 43, 49, 51, 55–6, 73, 79
Organisation of Petroleum Exporting Countries (OPEC) oil crisis 55

organizational change and economic performance 96–7
organizational forms, emergence of new 98
Osterman, P. 87, 89
output: indicators 37–40; prices, errors in measuring 48
output-over-all inputs index 13
outsourcing 41; foreign and domestic 47

Page, J.M., Jr. 24
Pakes, A. 38, 68
Panel Study of Income Dynamics (PSID) 90
Park, K.S. 85, 88
Parsons, D.J. 92, 95
partial factor productivity 23; indices 25, 42
patents 37, 101; as output indicator 38
Patterson, D.G. 29
Perloff, J.M. 25
Petit, M.L. 112, 114
Petit, P. 79
Phelps, E.S. 79
physical capital 2
physical technology 6
Physiocrats 16
Pindyck, R.S. 112
Pischke, J.S. 84, 91
plant and equipment, depreciation of 55
population growth 16
Porter, M.E. 112
post-productivity slowdown literature 50
post-Second World War: period 46; researchers 13
Poyago-Theotoky, J. 112, 115
Pralahad, C.K. 111–12
Prescott, J.E. 104
Prevezer, M. 69
price competition 60
private capital investment 17
private–private research partnerships 99–100
process-related innovations 61
producer: behavior 15; price index 47
product innovation 7, 18
production, factors of 9
production function 8–9; aggregate 10, 17, 23–5; concept of technological change 20; framework 25, 33; model 14, 90
production function-based measures of productivity 23–33

154   *Index*

production studies, microeconomic-based 50
productivity 8–10; growth 8–10, 14, 16, 42, 50–9, 76; index 13–14; slowdown 49
productivity-enhancing innovations potential 49
productivity-related variables, annual growth rates in 52
profit incentives, short-run 58
profitability 113
public policy, primary role of 5
public–private research partnerships 99–100
public technology-based institutions 100
purchased technology 61, 79

quality: change 47; of life 1; mismeasurement 50
quality-ladder theory 18
Quesnay, F. 2

Raa, T. 41
Ranis, G. 22
Rasche, R.M. 55
Rees, A. 50, 68–9, 78
Regev, H. 86, 90, 106
Reifschneider, D. 124
Reilly, K.T. 86, 89
Reinganum, J. 18
research: applied 66; basic 66; capital, stock of 18
research and development (R&D) 34, 36, 61, 101; activities 7, 49, 61, 63, 67–9; by character of use 66–7; and computers, external investments in 96; decline in rate of return 58–9; dimensions of 64; disaggregated, productivity growth studies of 75–8; effects of 91; embodied in purchased inputs 73; expenditures 37, 56, 73; foreign investments in 65; government-financed 73, 75; indigenous 78–9; intensity 91; investment 88; performers 65–6; and productivity growth, empirical evidence 72–8; projects 58; self-financed 75, 78; in small firms, literature related to 67; sources of funding 64–9; space-related 65; spending, industrial 73; spillovers, sources of 98; tax credits 74; unit, internal 62; in universities and colleges 65; worldwide post-slowdown policy 73–5

Research and Development Joint Ventures Act of 1983 116
research joint ventures (RJVs) 101, 115
research partnerships 76, 98–100, 102–19; role in generation of technologies 6
Research Triangle Part, North Carolina 40
resource allocation, efficiency of 1
Reuer, J.J. 104–5
Roberts, J. 96
Roberts, M.J. 33
Romeo, A. 39, 68
Romer, P.M. 16–18
Roosevelt, President F.D. 66
Rosenkranz, S. 112
Russia 64
Ruttan, V.W. 29

Sahal, D. 40
Sakakibara, M. 102
Sala-i-Martin, X. 18
Salter, W.E.G. 22
San Antonio 118
Sanchez, R.A. 112
Santoro, M. 109
Sato, R. 31
Saxenian, A. 69
scale economies, realization of 31
Schakenraad, J. 102
Schankerman, M.A. 37, 72–3
Schendel, D. 104
Scherer, F.M. 7, 37–8, 68, 72, 75–6
Schmitz, J.A. 85, 89–90
Schmookler, J. 13, 37–8
Schultz, T.W. 13
Schumpeter, J.A. 7–8, 17; phases in process of technological change 7
Schwalback, J. 68
science: base 63; parks 98
scientific knowledge 6
scientists, academic and industry 101
Scott, J.T. 38–40, 69, 99–100, 105
Second World War 3, 64–5
Semiconductor Industry Association (SIA) 115–16
SEmiconductor MAnufacturing TECHnology (SEMATECH) 117
Semiconductor Research Corporation (SRC) 115–16
Shane, S. 108
Shivakumar, R. 111–12
Sichel, D. 36, 92, 95–6
Sicherman, N. 83
Siegel, index of 26

Silicon System 116
Simpson, R.D. 111
skill-biased technological change (SBTC) 79–80; basic analytical framework of empirical studies 80–1; empirical studies of 81–91; literature 81, 92; theoretical models of 80; wage and employment implications of 88
Sleuwagen, L. 76
Small Business Innovation Research (SBIR) programs 101
small firms, economic importance of 67
small and medium-sized enterprises (SME) 67
Smith, A. 1–2, 15
society: benefits or returns from technological change 12; investments in R&D 12
Soesan, J. 41
Soete, L. 79
Solow, R.M. 13–15, 29, 31–2, 35, 80, 91; (1956) growth model 16–18; (1967) classification scheme 23; aggregate production-function model 14; Cobb–Douglas estimates 30; Divisia or geometric index 27; productivity paradox 92; residual measure of total factor-productivity growth 28
Southwest Research Institute 118
Soviet Union 43; space successes 65
spillover: effects 96; literature 68; mechanism 101
static (non-tournament) models with spillovers 114
Statistics Canada 66, 118
Steindel, C. 95
Stephan, P.E. 69
Stern, S. 96
Stevenson, R. 124
Stigler, G.J. 9–10, 76
Stiroh, K.J. 36, 93–6
stochastic frontier estimation (SFE) 124
stock: prices 101; of R&D capital 81
Stolarick, K.M. 93
Stoneman, P. 28
strategic management 111–12
strategic options 114
strategic research partnerships (SRPs) 118; evaluation of 101
Stuart, T.E. 104
Sudit, E.F. 24
Summers, R. 18–19
superconductors 76
Suzumura, K. 111

Swan, T.W. 15
Sweden 43
symbols, definition of 121–3
systems concept of technology 40

tangible tools 6
Tassey, G. 70, 78
Tatom, J.A. 55
tax policies specific to R&D in various countries 74
technical knowledge 25; early conceptual model of sources of 60–2
technical progress 14, 30; alternative frameworks for measuring 34
technological change 5–8, 17, 120; and economic performance 96–7; impact on economic activity 14; literature 20, 76; microeconomic determinants of 36; rate of 13
technological spillovers 99; *see also* spillover
technology 5–8; usage 89; wage premium 90
technology-intensive plants 89
technology–productivity growth relationship 70–1; literature 15
technology-related investment behavior 51
Teece, D.J. 112
Terleckyj, N.E. 72–3, 75–6
Texas 118
Thursby, J.G. 107
Thursby, M.C. 107
Tinbergen, J. 9–10
Tobin's *q* 55
Tokutsu, I. 95
Tolwinski, B. 112, 114
total factor productivity 10, 23, 42; annual growth rates 34, 44–5; growth index 9; growth slowdown 51; indices 27–34, 42; measurement 37
tournament models with no spillovers 114
Trajtenberg, M. 38
transactions cost 111; literature 113
Trigeorgis, L. 112
Troske, K. 90

undeveloped countries 42
unionization 57
United Kingdom (UK) 33, 43–4, 52, 65, 89–90
United States (US) 33, 36, 42–4, 50–2, 58, 64–5, 73, 89, 98; Bureau of Economic Analysis (BEA) 36; Bureau of Labor Statistics (BLS) 26, 89;

United States (US) (*Continued*)
  Census Bureau 81, 90; chemicals, machinery, and petroleum industries 56; data on productivity growth rates 45; economy 13–14, 32, 34, 45–6, 51, 54, 73, 76; industries, competitiveness in emerging technologies 77; manufacturing firms, R&D groups in 62; manufacturing industries 33, 41, 56, 88; National Innovation System 58, 65; private domestic economy 30; product, growth in 35; productivity growth, measurement error 46–8; productivity slowdown 51; R&D 65, 73, 77
United States Department of Commerce 77, 116; Advanced Technology Program 58, 100; Technology Administration of 76
university: spillovers 78; technology transfer 98; technology transfer office (TTO) 98
university-based entrepreneurial start-ups 98
university–industry technology transfer (UITT) 98
Usher, A.P. 8

van de Klundert, T. 30
Van den Broeck, J. 124
van Reenan, J. 74–5, 85, 89–91
Venkatraman, N. 104
Verdoorn, P.J. 50; Law 50

Veugelers, R. 111–12
vintage model, applications of 32
Vonortas, N.S. 105, 111–12, 114

Wachter, M.L. 25
wages: inequality between skilled and non-skilled workers 89; and innovation, panel data on 89; premium 89
Waldman, D. 98
Wallsten, S. 76, 107
Walters, A.A. 31
Watt–Boulton steam-engine venture 7
Welch, J. 79, 89
West Germany 42–4, 52
Williamson, O.E. 111
Winter, S.G. 24
Wolff, E.N. 26, 41, 93
work environment 97
Worker-Establishment Characteristic Database (WECD) 90
workers: categories of 81; highly educated 89; skilled and unskilled 91; white-collar 88
workhorse diffusion or logistic function model 38
Workplace Industrial Relations Survey (WIRS) 1984 90
world energy crisis 49

Ziedonis, A.A. 108
Zimmermann, K.F. 68
Zmud, R.W. 62
Zucker, L.G. 103